HeadTrash

**Cleaning Out the Junk
That Stands Between
You and Success**

*Tish Squillaro
and Timothy I. Thomas*

EMERALD
BOOK CO.

Published by Emerald Book Company
Austin, TX
www.emeraldbookcompany.com

Distributed by Emerald Book Company

For ordering information or special discounts for bulk purchases, please contact Emerald Book Company at PO Box 91869, Austin, TX 78709, 512.891.6100.

Design and composition by David Wilk of Booktrix and
Creative Management Partners LLC
Cover design by Jason Haker of Jason Haker Designs
Cartoons by Gene Schultz

Publisher's Cataloging-In-Publication Data
(Prepared by The Donohue Group, Inc.)

Squillaro, Tish.
  HeadTrash! : cleaning out the junk that stands between you and success / Tish Squillaro and Timothy I. Thomas.—1st ed.

   p. ; cm.

  Issued also as an ebook.
  Includes bibliographical references.
  ISBN: 978-1-937110-51-2

  1. Leadership—Psychological aspects. 2. Management—Psychological aspects. 3. Emotions. 4. Success in business. I. Thomas, Timothy I. II. Title.

HF5386 .S65 2013
658.4/094   2013930125

Part of the Tree Neutral® program, which offsets the number of trees consumed in the production and printing of this book by taking proactive steps, such as planting trees in direct proportion to the number of trees used: www.treeneutral.com

Printed in the United States of America on acid-free paper

13 14 15 16 17   10 9 8 7 6 5 4 3 2 1

First Edition

TreeNeutral

DEDICATION

To my loving parents, for raising me to be the woman I am, my two beautiful children, Berlyn and Jack and my husband and best friend, Matt, for not only their unconditional love and constant encouragement, but for helping me clean out my "trash" time and again. You are always my greatest inspiration!

And, a special thank you to Lisa (aka "Mrs. Leonard") for her devoted friendship, and for always being my biggest cheerleader!

—Tish

To my loving wife, Elaine, for her steadfast support in all seasons. Countless times throughout the years you have believed in me when I did not believe in myself and helped me to accomplish things I never dreamed I could. I am blessed to be your husband.

—Tim

CONTENTS

ACKNOWLEDGMENTS

Writing *HeadTrash* was a labor of love that would have been near impossible without the help of a group of wonderful professionals who gave of their time and expertise. We were blessed to work with Alan Sharavsky, whose counsel, wit, and ability to turn a phrase has added immeasurably to the text of the book. We are also grateful to the executives who from their vast storehouse of leadership wisdom and experience contributed to the "From the desk of:" sections of the book: Phil Clemens, Chairman and CEO Hatfield Quality Meats; Tim Myers, Liquid Hub Lead Partner; Peter Musser, Chairman and CEO of the Musser Group and Chairman Emeritus of Safeguard Scientific; Chris Saridakis, CEO of GSI Commerce; Marta Martinez, AOL Head of Sales Strategies and Operations; and Erika Weinstein, president of Stephen-Bradford Search.

We are also indebted to Hilary Hinzmann, who served us wonderfully as a thought-provoking editor who continually challenged us to be clear in our thinking and writing. We also wish to extend our gratitude for the creative genius of Jason Haker, our cover designer, and Gene Schultz, our illustrator, who continually amazed us with their skills and responsiveness. We would also like to acknowledge our friend and partner, Elliot Levine, whose wise counsel and support has helped us immeasurably in making this book immensely relevant and helpful to our readers.

Finally, we are grateful for all the business leaders who have had the courage to face their HeadTrash and do the courageous work necessary to transform their lives and their businesses.

Getting Unstuck

I know I can go farther in my career. But I've hit a plateau, and I'm not sure why.

I've always thought my employees were unmotivated grumblers. Now I'm thinking, maybe it's me.

I'm losing my best people left and right! They tell me they're frustrated. But what are they not telling me?

Senior management won't give me the authority to make decisions. If they don't believe in me, how can I believe in myself?

Storm Warning: It's Your Wake-Up Call

You're driving your team to a business meeting during a winter storm. The salt trucks haven't gotten to this part of the road yet. Everyone is crawling, trying to maintain momentum without sliding out of control. You become irritated by others' over-cautiousness and lack of speed. You see no need to adjust your driving to accommodate a little bit of snow. You're coming up to a red light, so you pump the brakes. As you reach the intersection, your car skids to a stop, just missing the car in front of you.

Your forward motion is gone, but at least you're in a safe spot and didn't hit anyone. You wait, the light changes to green, and you tap forcefully on the gas pedal. Your wheels start spinning; you're stuck in a quagmire of slush, ice, and snow! You press hard on the gas, spewing snow and ice and digging yourself into a deeper hole. The cars behind you are also stuck, their drivers fearful of what you'll do next. Yet the cars to the left and right of you are slowly making their way forward, including many you passed on the road earlier.

Why did *you* get stuck? Was it arrogance, assuming you could handle the weather and did not need to slow down? Insecurity about how your team might judge your driving? Or fear of the client's reaction if you are late for your meeting? You can't move forward, and you surely can't go back. You try again and again, but the wheels just spin. Every time you hit the gas, your team gets more nervous. Soon they're asking: *"Should we call a tow truck?" "Should we get out and push?" "If we can get going again, is there a better route to take the rest of the way?"* You're irritated, and you begin to worry that you won't get to your meeting at all. Missing the meeting will be bad. But maybe you've got a bigger problem junk in your head that is causing you to make poor decisions like driving without regard for the weather and road conditions or the attitude and opinions of your team.

Getting stuck on the snowy, icy road is typical of how your days have been going. You're expending energy, lots of it, but not making progress. Even though you're frustrated and know something is out of sync, you can't seem to change the situation. Each day you're becoming a little more anxious, which is making you less productive and more concerned about the future. You know something has to change. You're just not sure what it is.

Why do executives get stuck? Why do leaders sometimes find themselves pushing hard but not gaining traction? Frequently it's because they're working against themselves, defeating their best efforts with their own problematic thoughts and emotions.

What Exactly Is HeadTrash?

In this book, we refer to thought patterns and emotional tendencies that hinder your ability to respond to business issues in a productive and professional way as HeadTrash. Put another way, HeadTrash is the negative voice of your subconscious, engaging you in a deadly inner dialogue that only you hear, consciously or subconsciously, but which affects everything you say and do and everyone around you. HeadTrash is any pattern of self-defeating feelings and thoughts that leads you into trouble and keeps you stuck there. Even worse, depending on your level of responsibility and authority, the rest of your team or company gets stuck, too.

As consultants to leaders of businesses and organizations from start-ups to the Fortune 500, we've found that HeadTrash takes seven main forms. The demons that plague business leaders most frequently, causing them to get stuck personally and professionally, are:

fear **ARROGANCE**

Insecurity   CONTROL

Anger *Guilt*

paranoia

As business owners, advisers, and coaches, we've repeatedly witnessed these seven forces in action and helped leaders learn to manage them. Certainly there are other problematic tendencies in human emotional and mental patterns, but these seven are the most fundamental and dangerous. They are primal problems that can damage or even destroy your business and career.

Based on our work with thousands of leaders, we've discovered that different forms of HeadTrash can produce similar symptoms in organizations and can often overlap. You will have to probe beyond symptoms to identify the form(s) of HeadTrash you need to address. The examples we offer will help you do that.

Everybody feels afraid, insecure, guilty, and so on from time to time. That's normal. But when problematic thoughts and feelings become patterns in your life and consistently affect your decision making and leadership behaviors, they're HeadTrash that require cleanup on your part.

HeadTrash Cocktails

This book is divided into chapters focusing individually on each type of HeadTrash. But as we'll discuss, two or more varieties of HeadTrash often work in tandem to create potentially lethal "HeadTrash cocktails."

For instance, outward *arrogance* is often spurred by inward *insecurity*. *Fear* may lead a manager to be overly *controlling*. *Guilt* can result in *paranoia*. And so on.

"I'd like a shot of fear with an insecurity chaser."

It's All Between Your Ears—Or Is It?

HeadTrash starts between your ears, but unfortunately it doesn't stay there. In the following chapters, we'll review the specific effects that each type of HeadTrash has on you and your business. The chain of negative impacts from HeadTrash goes like this:

The Impact on You

Who's the first victim of your HeadTrash? You guessed right. It's you. In every case—whether you are acting out of fear, arrogance, insecurity, control, anger, guilt, or paranoia—your decision-making process and leadership behaviors are negatively affected:

Fear: You avoid taking action.
Arrogance: You ignore warning signs.
Insecurity: You—it's all about you.
Control: You refuse to let go.
Anger: You explode.
Guilt: You do things you know are wrong or don't want to do.
Paranoia: You always feel "they" (board, team, employees, investors) are out to get you.

The Impact on Your Employees

People find it extremely difficult to work under a leader who has serious HeadTrash problems. Think of the gripes you see on employee blogs:

"It drives me crazy—he just won't make a decision about *anything!*"

"He is so arrogant … and he doesn't even know what we do!"

"I'm tired of working nights and weekends on this when she's just going to change it anyway."

The complaints may differ, but the result is the same. Employees become more and more frustrated, and less and less productive, working under a leader who suffers from HeadTrash.

The Impact on Your Business

Frustrated employees are unhappy employees, disengaged and negatively affecting the company's performance. Do you have employees who:

Gripe, creating an unhappy, negative, dysfunctional culture;

Slack off, reducing overall productivity and compromising the quality of products and services;

Ditch the company, taking all their skills, expertise, and intellectual property with them; and

Badmouth the brand and company reputation through complaints and gossip?

The fact is, a business cannot move ahead when its people's behaviors are holding it back. The damage to net return shows up clearly year after year in the company's bottom line.

You Don't Have to Stay Stuck

While it may sound grim, you don't have to stay stuck. Here's the key to getting free:

> **HeadTrash has to do with how you think and how you act—and you can change both.**

Behavioral change is not about personality. Personality traits are intrinsic to the core of an individual; they're pretty much permanent. Whether you're introverted or extroverted, daring or cautious, a detail-oriented or a big-picture person, that's who you are, and it's not going to change.

HeadTrash, on the other hand, is about how you think and how you act. And guess who's in control of that? You are. Think of it this way:

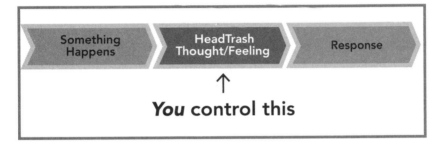

Case History: A New CEO Makes His First Big Decision

Dale is a newly installed CEO whose company stops doing business with a major account. A significant investor in the company subsequently calls and asks, "What happened with the Stykowski account?"

Dale snaps, "They wanted way too much from us. We could never please them!"

"I'm surprised," the investor says. "I thought you felt the account had great growth potential."

Dale snarls, "Look, I told you, we were bending over backwards for this client and it was starting to hurt our margins! We had to walk away to protect our business as a whole."

After the phone call, Dale can't let the matter rest. He begins to second-guess his decision and worry that the investor thinks his judgment is bad. Over the following two days Dale obsessively rehashes the scenario with the client account's team and twice phones the investor to assure him that they made the right decision, the second time with the client team leader on the call.

In truth, the investor was making a simple and legitimate inquiry—no condemnation intended. And Dale's decision to jettison the account, taken after a review he initiated of all the company's accounts showed that it had much less potential than he thought, as well as low current margins, was actually a sound business call. The review resulted in the jettisoning of several medium- to high-volume accounts with low margins and meager growth prospects, freeing the sales organization to concentrate resources on more profitable current and prospective accounts. However, Dale's inherent paranoia caused him to misread the conversation with the investor and then distract his entire team and himself at the same time. Not only that, Dale has now fulfilled his own worst-case scenario. He has raised serious doubts about his leadership in the mind of the investor, whose stake gives him considerable clout with the board of directors.

The key point is that the trigger for a problematic emotional response may be incredibly fleeting; it may happen at an unconscious level. Unfortunately, we often respond to situations based upon our emotions rather than on logical thought.

HeadTrash happens first at a subconscious level and then generates unhealthy and irrational mental and emotional patterns that in turn generate counterproductive behaviors. This leads to poor decisions and faulty management.

The good news is that you can learn to identify your HeadTrash and nip it in the bud. You can change your emotional responses, with the result being a new and successful behavior pattern. Changing habitual patterns of thinking and feeling is difficult, to be sure, but the tools to transform your HeadTrash are within your grasp. Success depends on your commitment to the process of dismantling counterproductive old habits and replacing them with productive new ones. We've seen many leaders succeed in doing this based on two factors.

Two Requirements to Get Unstuck: Awareness and Willingness

There are two simple but powerful requirements for getting unstuck: awareness and willingness. This book will help you with the awareness part of the equation. Instead of esoteric psychobabble, these pages offer practical guidelines to help you be a more effective business leader. We identify the characteristic scenarios of the different varieties of HeadTrash and how they mess up your decision making and leadership. We portray the impact each type of HeadTrash has on the people around you. Most important, we provide you with proven insights and practical techniques to clean up the junk that stands between you and success.

For example, one approach that we have used successfully in the past to help people like Dale is to encourage them not to assume what people are thinking, but instead to ask questions to clarify and better understand the message being sent. Rather than assume that his company's investor was attacking him and snapping back, Dale would have been wise to say, "I get the feeling you are concerned that I might have lost a valuable account unnecessarily. Is that true?" This would have allowed the investor to state that he was merely looking for information, not accusing Dale of something. That would in turn have allowed Dale to talk about the review of account profitability he had conducted, the strategic insight this provided, and the new agenda it gave the sales organ-ization. Thanks to Dale's lack of insight into and control over his HeadTrash, however, he snatched at least partial defeat from the jaws of victory and greatly complicated his relationship with the company's board of directors.

Even though we don't know who you are, we share a common goal with you. We want to see your career, your employees, and your business flourish. If that's going to happen, you have to be completely honest about where you stand right now.

That brings us to the second requirement for getting unstuck: willingness to change. This is something you have to supply. But we can help you locate it in your motivation to fulfill your potential and succeed in your business.

Will This Really Work?

Is it simple? Yes. Is it easy? Well, if it were, there would be no need for this book. As we've already said, changing ingrained habits will be hard, perhaps harder than anything you've ever done. But you can do it if you commit to the process and work on it day by day. And even partial success in changing bad habits to good ones can produce a return on your investment of time and effort that can transform your career and the rest of your life for the better. This is an arena where steady, modest improvement can generate significant benefits over the short, medium, and long term.

In fact, it's important to understand that it won't be possible to *eliminate* HeadTrash from your life entirely. We're all human, and contending with our foibles is part of our humanity. In some ways, it's similar to the challenge many people face trying to achieve and maintain a healthy weight. The first step is to stop fad dieting. The second step is to create a lifestyle change by eating sensibly and exercising regularly. Then will all the weight problems disappear? That depends on a lot of things, not all of which are under an individual's control, but the most important factor will be continued effort over the long term to sustain healthy diet and exercise habits. To turn back to career and business success, the most important factors in achieving positive change will be your own discipline and commitment.

While completely removing HeadTrash is not possible for any human being, this book will enable you to become more aware of your HeadTrash, reduce it, and work around it. You'll see (maybe for the first time) its effect on those around you. And then you'll be more capable of minimizing its effects on your decision-making process. If you're aware and willing, positive change is guaranteed.

And what a positive change! Living with lots of HeadTrash is exhausting, like a central processor–draining software program running in the back of your mind 24/7. You may not be consciously aware of your HeadTrash, or you may argue with it hour after hour, day after day. As you manage and clean up your HeadTrash, you'll free up a tremendous amount of mental and emotional energy that you can focus productively on your business.

Our HeadTrash "Aha" Moment

By way of background, we have been working together for over seven years as business advisers and leadership coaches focused on senior-level decision-making scenarios. Over coffee one day in 2009 we discovered a common thread among many of the challenges leaders face: mental and emotional barriers. As we defined what we describe in this book, we felt we had something important to share. To prove our hunch we spent the next three years testing HeadTrash cleanup and removal strategies and techniques and integrating them into our leadership training workshops and programs. There has been universal agreement among our clients that ill-managed HeadTrash can be very destructive to businesses and their leaders. Many leaders have asked us for a tool to help them navigate through their HeadTrash—a blueprint with techniques for both recognizing it and cleaning it up. We wrote this book with those requests in mind.

As coauthors we've used "we" throughout this book. But we add our individual two cents through "Tish Says" and "Tim Says" speech boxes.

We will regularly take you "behind the scenes" to share how we have worked with HeadTrash-challenged leaders. We're forever grateful for the chance to work with executives on issues that cut so close to the bone. We're in awe of the courage and honesty that these individuals showed in acknowledging and resolving their HeadTrash. And we'd love to honor the struggles and celebrate the successes of each and every one of them. As we've already said, HeadTrash is something every human being has, and anyone who feels holier than thou about HeadTrash is probably in a state of denial about the junk rattling around in his or her psyche. But in the interests of privacy for our clients and relevance for you, the examples you'll find here are composites of many real-life executives and companies. No example is based on or represents a single individual or a single company.

Last but not least, each chapter features "From the desk of:" contributions from senior executives with superb leadership track records who have found the HeadTrash concept relevant and true to their experience, especially in mentoring junior leaders. Their perspectives on successfully dealing with and averting HeadTrash offer valuable insights and inspiration for your own cleanup campaign.

Before we get started in earnest, let us offer one more thought about the need to address HeadTrash for your own benefit, if not that of others. We now and then run into executives who defiantly say, "Maybe I'm not easy to work for. Maybe I'm a jerk. But I get things done." Denying the need to deal with your HeadTrash is a dangerous thing to do. Sure, there are outliers who achieve great success despite having lots of HeadTrash. For example, it seems pretty clear from Walter Isaacson's bestselling biography of Steve Jobs that he could be unnecessarily harsh on others and appallingly arrogant. That didn't stop him from building one of the greatest companies of our time. If you're sure you're so good at what you do that your HeadTrash will not hurt you or your business, good luck! If you're not so sure, read on.

Fear—
Moving Forward Despite It

"I don't know how my colleagues do it. Personally, I think they're usually too quick to make decisions. I like to gather all the data and sit with it for a bit before pulling the trigger, especially on a big call. A lot of times while I'm analyzing, a new piece of information comes in, and I'm glad I wasn't so hasty. I can study all the evidence, pro and con, and then decide what's best. I've been criticized for delaying on some tough issues, but I don't want to do the wrong thing. My only thought is what's best for everyone involved."

—A Leader with Fear HeadTrash

Everyone can tell that Steve is in over his head. He's been a bad fit for the new role pretty much since the day you promoted him. You've been meaning to talk to him about it, to have the difficult conversation and make a personnel change. But there's no putting it off now. The latest person to have concluded the obvious is your largest client.

You just got off the phone, and her words are still ringing in your ears: "Nothing personal, but I'd be happier *if Steve were not running my account.*"

This is a sequential failure, a fiasco on two fronts that began with your refusal to deal with a difficult problem when it first arose, and then to make a tough decision. The no-decision decision led to irritating a major client. You still have a problem with Steve. And now you have a threat to your business as well.

Yet even now you can't bring yourself to have the talk, let alone switch a new person into the role.

What exactly is going on here? You might want to label it benevolence, being a humane boss and looking out for Steve's best interests. Or you might call it practical, not wanting to fire someone without a person of equal experience to replace him. But let's call it what it really is: fear.

And then, let's be honest about fear. It's prevalent, perhaps even omnipresent, in business because it plays such a big role in human experience and comes in so many forms. The *Merriam-Webster* online dictionary captures the wide spectrum of fear as follows:

> *fear* noun 1 *a:* an unpleasant often strong emotion caused by anticipation or awareness of danger. *b (1):* an instance of this emotion *(2):* a state marked by this emotion
> 2: anxious concern : SOLICITUDE
> 3: profound reverence and awe especially toward God
> 4: reason for alarm : DANGER

Why did Steve's manager wait so long to address an issue that was obvious to everyone, including him? It was because of fear—fear of being seen as the bad guy. The manager did not make the proper business move because Steve, a likeable, long-standing employee, would be devastated by the feedback that he was not performing well on the account. The manager's fear of having the difficult conversation has put the company in jeopardy.

Fear versus Caution:
Reflexive Flight versus Thoughtful Action

Fear is so hard to overcome because we humans are hardwired for it. Fear, after all, is the survival instinct, the impulse that prompted our ancient ancestors to flee when ugly creatures with big claws and teeth began picturing them as entrées. What could be more sensible than feeling fear when pondering an important personnel change, a major investment, a big presentation? The stakes are high, and fear in these circumstances is just common sense, right? Well, not exactly. Extreme fear often stops executives and managers cold. It's not a speed bump; it's a brick wall. It can render people incapable of taking action because they're too worried about the downsides. So nothing changes. Nothing improves. Nothing gets done.

Compare that with fear's nobler cousin, caution. In its third definition of caution, *Merriam-Webster* describes it as "prudent forethought to minimize risk."

Caution, in other words, recognizes that there really are risks to what we do in business—often large ones. It admits that there are many potential consequences to an action and that not all of them may be good. But caution takes a proactive point of view, considering the whole picture and how to minimize the hazards without losing sight of the upsides.

The expression "proceed with caution" generally captures the best way to handle fear, taking action with an appropriate level of respect for the potential negative outcomes. But before we can learn how to proceed with caution, we need to understand more about the two most common fears in business: fear of making the wrong decision and fear of having a difficult conversation.

"Courage is resistance to fear, mastery of fear—
not absence of fear."

—Mark Twain

Fear of Making Decisions: "What If I'm Wrong?"

Decision anxiety is not a phobia or a delusion. It's a normal and often valid response to reasonable concerns about how your judgments and actions can impact your business or career. Typically, these fears line up in three categories:

- *Fear of risk,* worrying that if things don't go well, you could lose a lot, including your reputation;

- *Fear of the unknown,* doubting that you have enough information to act; and

- *Fear of admitting ignorance,* the inability to admit you are not sure what to do.

As a leader *you're charged with making decisions and following through on them.* You're the one the rest of the staff turns to for guidance, direction, and strategy. Yes, the team provides information, feedback, input, and recommendations. But it's you, the leader, who must offer the vision and then encourage the team to go where they've never gone before.

Who wants to march into new territory behind an indecisive leader? No one rushes to line up behind the captain who says in a timid voice, "This is where we probably need to go, maybe." Or says nothing at all.

> *Tish Says: Remember NO decision is a decision, and it is usually a bad one.*

Fear of making the wrong decision can paralyze leaders into making no decision, taking a "safe" approach, which usually is no approach. Sadly, many leaders would rather stand still than risk making a move—even if staying put means losing sales, tolerating inefficiency, and bypassing opportunities. But in today's fast-paced world, if you're not evolving and getting better, you're probably getting worse.

Fear of Speaking Up: "I Can't Say *THAT!*"

If you're like most leaders, people problems are the ones that keep you up at night. And the most dreaded people problem of all is when an employee—especially one in a critical role—has to be confronted about unacceptable behavior or poor performance.

Fearful leaders have many tactics to avoid a difficult conversation:

- *Do nothing and hope the problem will resolve itself.* The most popular choice, but the least effective. Few personnel problems ever go away on their own.

- *Delegate the dirty deed to someone else.* Can you say "cop out"?

- *Issue a general reprimand to the group.* For example, rather than confront Ted on his lack of collaboration, his manager calls a general meeting or sends a team-wide e-mail urging everyone to collaborate more effectively. The results of such a move usually take three directions.

1. Most people know exactly what's going on—and resent the public scolding for something they didn't do. Further, they're angry that the manager has not addressed the problem directly with the offender, Ted.

2. A minority of people mistakenly think they're to blame, and they become worried and anxious.

3. Oblivious to the indirect rebuke, Ted does not change his behavior.

- *Soften the conversation too much.* Then there are the times when the fearful leader actually gets up the nerve and calls in an employee for a talk. But then the leader dances around the issue, minimizing it with such oblique, veiled language that the employee has no idea he or she has done anything wrong.

> *Tim Says: I know a manager has fear HeadTrash when I hear one of these timeworn excuses:*
>
> - *"I don't want to upset him because he'll leave the company!"*
>
> - *"I'm tired of always being the bad guy!"*
>
> - *"If I fire her, what will happen to the team's performance?"*

BEHIND THE SCENES WITH TISH & TIM:
FEAR ANECDOTE I—THE NON-RESULTS OF THE
SOFT APPROACH

We once encountered a classic case of the "soft approach" when working with a global manufacturer of medical devices that was installing new customer relationship management (CRM) software in its sales organization. The company had just acquired three companies in Europe and needed more transparency and consistency in their sales data and communication across the combined operations. Installing the CRM represented a major change for the company, as they had never had such a formal sales and relationship management system. The complicating factor in instituting this change was that the vice president for sales had long been friends with one of her direct reports. The two of them had been together with the company from its inception, which made it difficult when this manager ignored the software and didn't insist on its use on his team. We recommended that the VP confront the issue head on. She agreed to do so.

A few days later, Tim followed up with the manager. The conversation went something like this:

> Tim: "How's that new sales tool going?"
> Manager: "Oh, fine!"
> Tim: "I spoke with the VP earlier, and she was concerned because your group wasn't using it as planned. It seems that your people haven't really bought in to it. Did she chat with you about it?"
> Manager: "Oh, she was a little annoyed with me, but I said my staff and I would use it once a week, and she said that was fine."

Now, in point of fact, the VP was more than a little annoyed. She was downright furious! It was *not* okay for the sales CRM software to be used just once a week. So Tim went back to the VP and told her, "Either I've lost my mind, or you have not delivered the message you said you'd like to deliver. You've clearly softened the message so that this manager doesn't realize the importance of using this software daily. Your conversation left this manager thinking, 'It's no big deal.' You need to address the severity of the issue *directly* with this manager." Sadly, it took multiple conversations before the VP gave the manager the appropriate feedback without softening it so much that it was ineffectual. This cost the company significant time, effort, and money.

Once the message had been delivered directly enough, however, the desired sales behaviors ensued. Consistent and disciplined use of the software provided accurate data that allowed for more realistic pipeline and forecasting reports, a deeper understanding of current client needs, and a higher visibility for all team members of sales activities with prospects and clients. Ultimately, the organization began to hit its marks in a much more efficient, effective, and profitable way for the company.

A Fear Checklist and Comparison

Which column sounds more like you?

A FEARFUL LEADER...	A COURAGEOUS LEADER...
Avoids confronting poor performance by ignoring it, stalling, or other "work arounds."	Will have the difficult conversation with employees about poor performance.
Reticent to try new initiatives because of the potential negative effects of change.	Will embrace new initiatives and drive change despite resistance by setting clear expectations.
Will not stand up for something if it is not fully accepted by others.	Will take a stand and attempt to influence others who might not be initially aligned.
Hires individuals who can easily be controlled.	Hires a very diverse team that brings a variety of perspectives and talents.
Can become paralyzed in the face of a difficult decision for fear making a mistake.	Recognizes that failure sometimes happens, but decisiveness is critical to success.
Will not admit ignorance or uncertainty for fear of looking weak and incapable.	Is comfortable admitting ignorance or uncertainty and will rely on team members' knowledge, skills and experience to solve problems.

HeadTrash Alert! A Quick Quiz on Fear

Please rate yourself on the following statements by placing a checkmark in the appropriate column:

	Never	Sometimes	Often	Always
I am afraid to have difficult conversations.				
I find myself repeatedly imagining worst-case scenarios about what might happen if I make a decision.				
I find myself obsessing over the same business issues repeatedly.				
I put off decisions under the guise of "needing more data."				
I will settle for the status quo, even when I know it's hurting the business.				
I accept questionable be-haviors from employees in roles that are critical to the business.				
I struggle with executing decisions that might make me look like the bad guy.				

If you checked "often" or "always" three or more times, you probably suffer from fear HeadTrash.

No Decision Is Usually the Worst Decision

If you still think it's better to do nothing rather than to risk a catastrophically wrong decision, consider this. Indecision is potentially the most catastrophic decision you can ever make. When a leader consistently refuses to take action, it sets up a triple whammy. The leader:

1. *Loses respect.* People no longer trust his or her judgement.
2. *Loses credibility.* People no longer trust his or her competence to lead the company.
3. *Loses trust.* People no longer believe that he or she can deliver on promises.

Getting others to follow your lead productively depends on continuing respect, credibility, and trust. When leaders lose these assets, their ability to take any effective action is in doubt.

> *Tish Says: As a leader, you must be decisive. People are watching and analyzing everything you do. Ultimately, you are only as good as people think you are.*

Good leaders set boundaries, engaged employees welcome them.

Think about what great leaders do on a daily basis:

- Establish a strategic vision and plan for achieving it,

- Set expectations and hold people accountable,

- Communicate the amount of risk taking that is desired and acceptable,

- Model how crisis situations are to be handled.

These are all different ways of establishing the boundaries within which the business operates. They require a leader to make decisions and to enforce them when necessary. If that happens consistently, people know where they stand, trust where they're going, and strive to get there. The leader's decisions and example channel their employees' energy like a swiftly flowing river.

But when a leader avoids making important decisions or setting necessary guidelines, energy sooner or later dissipates. Like water overflowing a river's banks, energy spills out wastefully or destructively. Employees then become:

- *Aimless.* Because management avoids strategic decisions, productivity grinds to a halt.

- *Frustrated.* People become desperate for *any* decision to be made—and care less and less about what the decision is. They just want *some* direction.

- *Disengaged*. With no direction or motivation, employees become clock-punchers. They show up, but that's it. Productivity plummets.

> *Tim Says: Thirty years of research by leadership experts James M. Kouzes and Barry Z. Posner reveal that people most want leaders who are honest, forward looking, competent, and inspirational. Fear derails every one of those four characteristics.*

Complacency and Your Competition

It won't surprise you that aimless, frustrated, and disengaged employees often don't stick around. In fact, the best employees—the smart, talented, experienced, and ambitious players you were hoping to promote—are usually the first out the door.

The ones who do stay slowly become numb. With no decisions being made, nothing ever changes. Complacency sets in, and the next sound you hear is the death knell of your business.

> *Tish Says: Becoming complacent about the status quo is the number-one killer for all businesses. Your competitor is not complacent! To keep the energy going, you have to overcome your fear of breaking the status quo: be different, be creative, address problems, and take risks!*

Surprise! You probably know what to do.

BEHIND THE SCENES WITH TISH & TIM:
FEAR ANECDOTE II—BEING NICE IS NOT ALWAYS NICE IN THE END

The irony about fear is that in most cases paralyzed leaders actually know what needs to be done. It's not confusion or ignorance holding them back, it's just fear. As the following example demonstrates, withholding painful but honest and appropriate feedback helps no one, including the employee.

We once worked with a senior director at a call center for a mid-sized distribution company, whom we will call Frank. Frank had a diverse team of four people working for him. Frank worked very well with two of them because he had been in their roles before hiring them. The other two employees he pretty much ignored because he was not as familiar with their area of the business and feared that interacting with them might expose his lack of knowledge. As a result, Frank provided very little direction to these employees and their performance suffered. At the time, we were working with Frank's manager, Julia. We argued that Frank was really losing the value of the two people he was ignoring, and that it would be best to split up the four people under him, let Frank keep the two he worked well with, and reassign the other two to a new manager.

But Julia resisted this move for six months. She had a long history with Frank, and didn't want to hurt him by confronting him on the issue and making the reassignment. We told Julia, "Frank is going to fail because his behavior is hurting the productivity of the entire group, and someone—like your boss—is going to make the decision for you to move the team around or possibly fire Frank. So what would you rather have happen? Do you want to be proactive and realign the team, or do you want someone else to make that decision?"

Ultimately, Julia's boss made the decision for her and restructured the team, taking the two direct reports ignored by Frank and assigning them to another manager in the department where they received direction that enabled them to thrive and increase their work output. As usual when leaders fail to address their HeadTrash, Julia's inability to resolve her fear of having the difficult conversation resulted in a cascade of unintended consequences. It negatively affected the two direct reports Frank was ignoring, until they were reassigned. It did Frank no favors with Julia's boss and left him twisting in the wind while his team continued to underperform. And it damaged her own credibility as a leader.

Re: Fear
From the desks of: Phil Clemens, Chairman and CEO
Hatfield Quality Meats and Tim Myers, Liquid Hub Lead
Partner, Financial Services and Insurance

According to Phil Clemens and Tim Myers, two corporate leaders who pretty much have seen it all while successfully guiding large companies for decades, fear wears a lot of disguises in business.

"Fear is one of the greatest limitations on leaders," says Myers. "Fear is really the leadership problem I see most often. Fear is everywhere. It takes so many forms and is often at the root of a number of counterproductive behaviors. Another problem with fear is that its nuances are sometimes hard to pinpoint. When you say 'fear,' some people may be afraid of losing $100 million. Well, that's a big fear. But I might also be afraid of going into the boss's office to ask for a raise because he might say no. I might be afraid of collaborating on work because I won't get credit. Fear is an interesting thing because it has so many occasions and guises."

For example, says Clemens, some executives fool themselves by mistaking hesitation for thoroughness. "Paralysis by analysis is rampant in the business world. Leaders keep thinking that if they just wait, they'll get that all-important piece of data. But often the more information we have, the harder it is to make decisions."

Clemens points out that fear is hardly limited to the executive suite. He sees it every day in politics, and points out how it influenced history. "If you go back to World War II and look at Neville Chamberlain and his inability to make decisions, my guess is it had a lot to do with fear HeadTrash. Fortunately, Winston Churchill came in and he didn't allow HeadTrash to take him off track. Without Churchill's decisiveness in those years, today's world would be very different."

How do seasoned leaders like Clemens and Myers deal with fear in the work place? How have they confronted this invisible enemy of growth and confidence? In a group setting, one effective method is to name it. Bringing fear out into the open renders it less powerful.

"The good news is you can address it. You can show people the value of a vision, and that there is nothing to be afraid of. It takes time, but being aware of fear allows you to get the work done, as opposed to not dealing with something that blows up later," says Myers.

And sometimes, it's a personal challenge, where you learn to listen for your own HeadTrash and act accordingly. Meyers says, "I may have to push certain thoughts to the back of my mind, because they're not a reality. If I let them become a reality and something I live by, then I can't make any forward progress."

Clemens points to Abraham Lincoln as a leader who valued decisiveness and action, appointing Ulysses S. Grant as general-in-chief of the Union Army. Why did Lincoln like the often unpopular and rogue commander? "Because he was not afraid to make a decision, even a wrong decision, in contrast to the generals who came to Lincoln and said, 'We can't do that.' Lincoln wanted a general who told him what he *could* do. Grant made some huge blunders, but he kept moving forward," says Clemens.

Clemens sums it up this way: "If I want to live in constant fear, then I do nothing. And doing nothing is not an option in business."

Recommendations for Overcoming the HeadTrash of Fear

TAKE A DEEP BREATH. TAKE IT SLOW. BUT TAKE ACTION.

Ultimately the only cure for the fear of making a wrong decision or the fear of having the difficult conversation is to just do it. Here are seven practical tools to make it easier for you:

1. *Build up to the big decisions.*
   If you've been frozen by fear, your decision-making muscles have atrophied. Don't put too much strain on them all at once. Start by making smaller decisions that are less frightening. Be consistent; that's the only way that real change will take place. Over time, you'll gain the confidence you need to make the big decisions that previously seemed impossible.

   A word of warning: avoid swinging to the other side of the pendulum—going from indecisive to impulsive. Stay committed to dealing with each situation calmly and rationally as it comes your way.

> *Tim Says: The worst of the pain usually passes within thirty-six hours—so stick it out for those thirty-six hours! Yes, those thirty-six hours will be intense, but it's far better than the alternative: dealing with the same problems for months or even years.*

> *Tish Says: Let me add this: you should be on-site for those thirty-six hours. Don't deliver your message and then ditch and run!*

2. *Accept the discomfort.*

   A lot of fear stems from knowing that certain decisions will result in upheaval, anger, distractions, or loss of key contributors. Accept it, and prepare yourself. But don't assume that pain equals a wrong decision, because nothing could be further from the truth.

   Before you start analyzing the results, wait until the dust has settled. The real outcome of a decision may not be apparent for days, weeks, or even months.

3. *Expect to make mistakes.*

   It's hard to accept, but here's the harsh truth: No one is perfect. Not us, not you, not the best leader you've ever worked with. There will be times you'll make a decision, and it will be wrong. Or you will have a difficult conversation, and totally blow it. Don't let this stop you from getting up, dusting yourself off, and trying again.

   Mistakes may make your gut churn, but here's the good news: People don't expect perfection. If your people see you weighing all the data and making a decision with confidence, they will respect and follow you. And that includes times you are proven wrong—as long as you promptly admit it, and then act with decisiveness and confidence to rectify the situation.

4. *Put your imagination to good use.*

   Your imagination can either help or hinder you in dealing with your fear. You can imagine a worst-case scenario and re-play it time and again in your head, sending your adrenaline spiking and your heart racing.

   Alternatively, you can imagine the worst-case scenario but look at it in the cold light of reason. Acknowledge that it could happen and decide what you will do if it does. This will allow you to be, if not comfortable with the possibilities, at least ready with an alternative action plan in your pocket.

5. *Seek third-party assistance when necessary.*

   There may be times when you need to call on third-party assistance to help you work through your fears about specific decisions you need to make. That third party may be:

   • A spouse or friend if you just need some emotional encouragement and support;

   • A business consultant if you need objective, professional guidance and direction;

   • A counselor or psychologist if your fears are deep-seated enough to incapacitate you even after you have made a serious effort at working through them.

Tish Says: A good business consultant will hold your feet to the fire until you make the decision you need to make!

6. *Accept that reality isn't always pretty.*

There are going to be situations that don't have nice, neat answers. For example, suppose you're a VP in a family-owned business, and the owner's incompetent son leads a department that reports to you. Can you fire him, even though he deserves it? Probably not.

But that doesn't mean you should do nothing. You might choose to take steps to strengthen the management team under him. Or you might put boundaries in place to make sure the department runs smoothly. Regardless, the point is the same. You should always do something rather than let a problem fester.

7. *Live in the present.*

Don't live in the past, but learn from it. Sure, you might have made some bad decisions in the past, but you've gained in wisdom and experience since then. Use your knowledge to avoid making the same mistakes again.

Don't live in the future. You can drive yourself crazy with all the "what-ifs." The things you are afraid of may come about. If they do, then you have a new decision to make: how to move forward.

Live in the present. Remember that courage is acting in spite of your fear. And as you act—as you make the necessary decisions, as you have the difficult conversations—your fear will never have control over you again.

2

Arrogance—Climbing Down from Your High Horse

> "I hate being right all the time, I really do. But I have to say what's on my mind, and sometimes I have to say it forcefully because I feel my point of view isn't always respected. It's not that I'm insecure, or need validation; it's that I know what's best for this company. I also know how to speak my mind. That's a sign of a good leader, right?"
>
> —A Leader with Arrogance HeadTrash

As vice president of engineering, you are leading a meeting regarding a major product rollout. There are thirty people in the room from around the globe, each with specific subject matter expertise. One of your colleagues makes a point during the meeting with which you disagree. You politely rebut the point. But because there are so many people talking, your opinion gets lost in the shuffle, and the discussion moves on.

Feeling that your observation didn't get its moment in the sun, you repeat yourself. This time the people in the room give you cursory acknowledgement, but the meeting proceeds full speed ahead.

Finally, possessed by your conviction that your comment requires more than a polite nod, you stand up, slam your hand on the conference table, and shout, "This is important because *I say* it's important!"

The meeting stops dead in its tracks. You think that is good news, because it forces everyone to recognize your rebuttal. It gets the attention it deserves, and so do you—but not necessarily in the way you imagine.

The others in the room are certainly impressed, so much so that the whole momentum of the meeting is lost. People stop sharing their ideas and all collaboration disappears. Not only that, your *exact words* soon echo around the company behind your back. In fact, your outburst becomes so notorious that a few of your peers and superiors secretly plot ways to keep you *out* of many key meetings from that point forward.

Here is *Merriam-Webster's* definition of arrogance:

arrogance *noun*:
an attitude of superiority manifested in an overbearing manner or in presumptuous claims or assumptions.

The synonyms for arrogance include haughtiness, insolence, and disdain. (When you see a positive word here, let us know.) But arrogance requires no formal definitions, because people who work with an arrogant leader have their own: "Egomaniac," "Know-It-All," "Jerk."

In short, there's absolutely nothing admirable about arrogance. It has no redeeming qualities.

Ego versus Egomania

While we're defining things, it might help to make an important distinction. Ego and arrogance are not synonyms. In recent years, ego has taken a bad rap. Consider the following colloquialisms:

- "She is a complete and total egomaniac."

- "He has such an inflated ego!"

- "She's so egocentric—everything has to revolve around her!"

All the above terms refer to ego gone haywire. But ego in and of itself is not negative. *Merriam-Webster* offers several definitions, including "the self of an individual person," "the conscious mind," and "one's image of oneself."

A healthy ego is essential to a balanced and happy life. Put simply, the "ego" is the "I," or the self. And since we all need a sense of our identity, an awareness of our conscious mind, and a sturdy self-image, a strong ego is a good thing. Ego becomes a problem when our "I" grows out of proportion, and we think the universe revolves around us.

> *Tish Says: Having a strong ego is a good thing—it's letting your ego rule without regard for anyone or anything else that wreaks havoc.*

"I see myself capable of arrogance and brutality.... That's a fierce thing, to discover within yourself that which you despise the most in others."
                    —George Stevens, director and screenwriter

Arrogance: The Personal Blind Spot Others Can't Miss

Glaringly obvious to everyone else, arrogance raises the question of why those who have it can't see it. The first explanation is that arrogance can be a mask for insecurity and defensiveness. In that case, arrogant leaders are trying desperately to overcompensate for low self-esteem. Plagued by internal demons, it's impossible for them to recognize or admit the ramifications of their external actions.

Since we'll address insecurity and defensiveness in the next chapter, we want to focus here on the second reason that arrogant people don't recognize that their arrogance is a problem. *Many leaders actually feel that it's a positive management trait.* They justify it. Condescending, self-important, overbearing? Hardly! Instead, they characterize themselves as confident, decisive, take-charge people who appropriately fill a leadership vacuum. No one does psychological spin better than arrogant leaders. After all, they have too much at stake.

BEHIND THE SCENES WITH TISH & TIM: ARROGANCE ANECDOTE I—SILENCE IS GOLDEN

We once worked with a rapidly growing 250-employee software company that was undergoing a major change initiative. The company had just replaced the top tier of leadership but kept the existing VP management structure. Emotions were running high. Uncertainty was rampant across the company. We felt it was important for the new CEO to show employees that their opinions mattered, so we established a series of "Breakfast with the Boss" meetings. During the first meeting, fifteen employees from all levels of the organization were present, and the CEO's job—his *only* job—was to listen to his new team's concerns and gain their insights regarding the challenges facing the company. As the meeting began a nervous employee asked the CEO a question. But instead of tossing the question back to hear the employees' thoughts on the subject, the CEO ran with it—for *forty-five minutes* of solid monologue. Then he adjourned the meeting, sincerely thinking it was a huge success.

Arrogant leaders usually talk more than they listen, thinking that being opinionated equals being viewed as confident. Members of any team or organization want confident leaders. But they do *not* want arrogant leaders who refuse to listen!

Arrogance from the Inside: Seek Honestly, and Ye Shall Find

Since it's hard to admit or see your own shortcomings, let's take a look from the inside. Do you often have thoughts like the following?

- "I told them!"

- "How dare they question me?"

- "What do they know?"

- "Do I have to think of everything around here?"

- "Nobody ever comes up with anything new."

- "I hired these people—why aren't they doing anything?"

If so, you may need to do some self-evaluation, but it won't come easily. We know that from personal experience.

BEHIND THE SCENES WITH TISH & TIM: ARROGANCE ANECDOTE II—BEFORE AND AFTER

On one occasion, we were hired by the CEO of a venture-backed alternative energy company that had just received its first round of funding. The business needed to grow from an entrepreneurial start-up to a more sustainable business model. It was the CEO's job as directed by his new investors to put into place processes and systems to bring the company to the next level. When we arrived for our first meeting at the company, the CEO greeted us with a rant about the staff: "I don't understand why they won't listen to me. Don't they know I know this business better than anyone? Why don't they bring me in on the tough decisions? Who do they think they are? I want you to fix those #*&^%* employees!"

After a little exploration, it became clear that the employees weren't the cause of the company's difficulty in growing to the next level. The CEO was the true source of the most serious problems, especially as it pertained to being open to others' ideas.

We began coaching to help the CEO work through his Head-Trash, which he was dumping on his employees day after day. He had HeadTrash of more than one variety, but arrogance was his biggest flaw. After several months of coaching he said, "Talking with you is like going to the dentist without novocaine. It's painful." But to his credit, he did the hard work of facing his arrogance. As a result, his entire approach to his team changed—he allowed open conversation and debate and welcomed his team's ideas and input. Over time the company was able to scale up and the CEO became a positive influence for change as opposed to its primary obstacle.

An Arrogance Checklist and Comparison

Which column sounds more like you?

AN ARROGANT LEADER...	A HUMBLE LEADER...
Is overly proud. She's certain she knows what she's doing, and does not invite help.	Is modest, and is willing to seek alternate opinions, asking, "What do you think about this approach?"
Feels threatened easily. His way is the best way. In fact, the only way!	Welcomes other people's ideas and input, and is eager to endorse another's idea.
Focuses on "I," even as he pretends to be interested in others. "So, let's talk about you. What did you think of my proposal?"	Focuses on "you." "Tell me about yourself, and what your goals are for this role."
Looks for ego stroking. "Wasn't the presentation I just did fantastic?"	Looks for constructive feedback. "That presentation went well, but I'd like to know how I could improve it."
Seeks power for the sake of power. "I deserve to be at the top because I am the best."	Seeks leadership for the sake of the bigger picture. "I want the best for this company and all the people who are part of it."
Uses people. "I will do what it takes to get to the corner office on the top floor."	Cares for people. "People are not projects, obstacles, or rungs on a ladder."

HeadTrash Alert! A Quick Quiz on Arrogance

Please rate yourself on the following statements by placing a checkmark in the appropriate column:

	Never	Sometimes	Often	Always
I find myself thinking, "Nothing happens around here without me."				
I have difficulty publicly admitting that I am wrong.				
People avoid me when they should be seeking my counsel				
I think it is a good thing when people feel nervous around me.				
I reject, attack, or twist other people's ideas so I can get my way.				
I regularly cut people off during conversations.				
I find it difficult to compromise for the greater good.				
I find it difficult to delegate power and authority.				

If you checked "often" or "always" three or more times, you probably suffer from arrogance HeadTrash.

Turning A-players into B-players:
Invisible Demotions and Dismissals

Arrogant leaders are extraordinarily good at hiring A-players for their teams, and no wonder. They view themselves as the best, so they want to hire only the best. Thus, they surround themselves with strong, smart, skilled individuals.

Unfortunately, the very arrogance that helps them handpick excellent employees quickly turns against them—and against their employees—in a one-two-three punch.

PUNCH ONE: EMPLOYEE FRUSTRATION

A primary role of any leader is to *motivate* his or her employees. But arrogant leaders do just the opposite: they *demotivate* and *frustrate* their employees. Their arrogance demands that no opinion except their own counts, that no procedure except their own can possibly work, and that no project is worthwhile unless it is their brainchild.

The result? The highly intelligent and talented employees are essentially forbidden to apply themselves. And nothing frustrates an A-player more than standing around while someone else hogs the ball. Soon you can kiss those all-stars goodbye.

PUNCH TWO: EMPLOYEE COMPLIANCE

Along with motivation, a true leader creates a culture of engagement. Arrogant leaders, however, create a culture of compliance by engaging in the following behaviors:

They reprimand employees (often in public) for challenging their opinions and ideas.

They modify every document, plan, or procedure in order to "make it perfect."

They require that all approvals or decisions cross their desk.

Ultimately, talented employees throw up their hands in despair and say, "I'll just do it the boss's way! I'm tired of putting out effort and having it thrown back in my face!" And then if at all possible they start planning to leave for a better environment with a leader who appreciates what they can do and gives them freedom to do it.

PUNCH THREE: EMPLOYEE SELF-DOUBT

The arrogant leader is never troubled by self-doubt. But he can sure instill it in his employees, eroding confidence in their own abilities. Constantly being told their ideas are not good, their opinions are invalid, their concerns are irrational, and their work is unsatisfactory, many eventually will come to believe it. This is the final step in the process of turning A-players into B-players, if they haven't already left you.

BEHIND THE SCENES WITH TISH & TIM: ARROGANCE ANECDOTE III—THE UNENTHUSIASTIC STAFF

We will always remember a client who exemplified the turning A-player into B-player syndrome. This person was the CEO of a professional services business that helped companies in the life sciences industry with strategic planning. He held himself in very high esteem, intellectually and professionally. As a result, nothing his staff did was ever right. Every plan that crossed his desk required the scrawl of his red pen. He typically handed back the modified document with a tight smile and said in a condescending manner, "*Now* it's better!"

By the time we met him, significant damage had been done to the company and its employees. There was no chitchat in the office. No interchange of ideas. No energy. No engagement.

Staff members with years of experience were constantly second-guessing themselves. "Can I write this report?" "Did I cover all the details for this event?" "Maybe I *can't* do anything right."

As for the leader, he was so far over the line when it came to his arrogance that he saw nothing wrong with the situation. Unfortunately, this leader's arrogance could not be overcome, and the way the business survived was for him to hire junior employees who would put up with his arrogance and "mentoring." Eventually the best of these young employees grew up (i.e., got very frustrated) and left the company. This model was not sustainable and was an emotional drain on the business. Had the leader managed his arrogance HeadTrash better, the company probably would have enjoyed more success.

The Arrogance Trap: Do You Really Want to Do It All?

Do you *truly* want to be responsible for every single thing that goes on in your office? Do you always want to feel like you have to pull people along, and do the thinking for them? Surely that's not why you hired all these talented people in the first place, so you could continue the herculean task of carrying the entire organization on your back.

That's why arrogance is always self-defeating. While it can be exhilarating in the short run to stand at the center of your own universe, it's draining in the long run. Sooner or later the arrogant leader becomes mentally exhausted from constantly doing the thinking for the entire team or department.

Stunted Growth

There's something else you should be aware of. There is a high likelihood that your arrogance will stunt your career growth.

Yes, you've gone far, climbed that ladder to get to where you are today. So why should you worry? Well, your arrogance will catch up with you, if it hasn't already. Eventually, your superiors will not promote you further. You already may have been uninvited to key meetings. And there might be no place for you on the board.

Why? Arrogance makes you unreliable—a potential loose cannon. Senior management can't afford to have you blow up in a meeting, insult an important client, or offend investors.

If you want to make it to the very top, it's time to deal with your HeadTrash.

Symptoms of an Arrogant Leader

If the above consequences haven't convinced you of the importance of addressing arrogance head on, consider the cost to your business.

- Your A-players don't like being treated like B-players. Eventually, they will leave, robbing you of the top talent your company needs to grow.

- Arrogance at the top validates the old proverb that "pride goes before a fall." Think about Bear Stearns, Lehman Brothers, Enron, and Bernie Madoff. Need we say more?

- When discussing business strategy and key decisions, people tend to avoid offering input or perspective if it differs from that of the arrogant leader. Smart people know fighting with a blockhead is a losing proposition.

- The arrogant leader's opinion tends to prevail, even if it is to the detriment of the company. Thus the company doesn't get the benefit of divergent points of view.

- In his book *The No Asshole Rule*, Robert Sutton, professor of management science at Stanford University, discusses the case of a successful software company that held onto one of its most arrogant leaders for far too long. The company calculated that the annual cost to keep this offender was $160,000.*

While we acknowledge there are some leaders who succeed with appalling levels of arrogance, unless you are truly a Steve Jobs–level player your arrogance will almost certainly wind up hurting your company's bottom line—and your career.

Arrogance versus Confidence

Arrogant people appear supremely self-confident, and therein lies the problem. Instead of having an appropriate level of confidence, they've crossed the line into arrogance. "Steve is the smartest person in the room. Just ask him!" Again, if you're Steve Jobs–level, that may work for you. Or it may lead to your career being ruined before you can climb to the top.

Truly confident people rarely cross over the line, because they don't need to tell everybody how wonderful they are. A confident leader has the strength and wisdom to be humble.

*Robert I. Sutton, *The No Asshole Rule: Building a Civilized Workplace and Surviving One That Isn't* (New York: Business Plus, 2007), 47.

Re: Arrogance
From the desk of: Peter Musser, Chairman and CEO of the Musser Group and Chairman Emeritus of Safeguard Scientific

Any entrepreneur would be proud to say he played a role in helping launch multiple Fortune 500 businesses. That's a credit that Pete Musser, CEO of the Musser Group, can lay claim to. A veteran of the technology and financial industries, Musser played an active role in the early stage development of QVC, Comcast, and Novell, Inc.

In truth, Musser's had so many successes and overcome so many challenges, he'd have the right to be a bit cocky. Yet mention arrogance, and Musser's perpetually positive disposition darkens. "I just can't stand arrogance," Musser says, grimacing. "When I see business arrogance, it makes me mad. It's not productive."

After over half a century in business, Musser not only can spot an arrogant executive, he can identify the type of arrogance the person has. For example, there is the "Smartest Guy In The Room" conceit.

"These people can be very bright; but they think they're brighter than everyone else. They might have a history of being smart, measured in school through good grades or being the leader of the class. And then, for the rest of their life, they have to prove it in every meeting."

This violates one of Musser's fundamentals for success. "I love the old saying, 'You never learn when you're doing all the talking.' I was always enough of a salesman to know I had to stop and ask a question or two. It's give and take. That's the key to successful communication."

For a person whose credentials qualify him to hold court, Musser recommends exactly the opposite. "Don't try to overwhelm the other person. Don't assume you know it all. If you can get others to talk, you can learn something that might be useful."

Another form of arrogance that rankles him is the "Power Tripper," the person who goes out of his way to demonstrate who's in charge. To make his point, he shares a story: "I saw three people get ushered into the conference room next to my office. I kept waiting for someone to come and meet them. A half hour went by, and they're still sitting in this conference room. So I went in and introduced myself.

"I found out they came in from Dallas the previous day. So obviously, this was an important meeting for them. I asked why they were here, and they gave me the name of the person they were meeting. I stayed there and chatted with them, and fifteen minutes later the guy finally shows up. He muscles in, very self-important, and says, 'Well, let's get started here. I don't have much time.' He was going to brush these people off, with me sitting right there! So I said, 'Gentlemen, I have plenty of time. Make your presentation. If he leaves, that's fine. I'm staying.' Well, we fired him, and I don't think he ever recognized exactly why that happened."

Ignorance and arrogance seem to go hand in hand. In fact, Musser feels that lack of self-awareness is the enemy of all leadership. "We know that the whole theory of management is that you're supposed to have a self-review meeting every month or so. We also know that nobody does it." And that, says Musser, is a crying shame. He feels that a leader's job is to be aware of his own foibles, and to help others work through theirs. "It's a great weakness if a person doesn't have self-awareness."

Recommendations for Overcoming the HeadTrash of Arrogance

Arrogant leaders focus exclusively on climbing *up*. Up the corporate ladder, up and over people, up to the top. But to overcome arrogance, your goal is actually to climb *down* off your high horse. Down to the level of your peers and employees and your common humanity, to a more mature and realistic view of yourself. You were probably uncomfortable sitting up there all alone anyway.

Here are six tools and tips to help you make that climb down, keeping in mind that your descent from arrogance will actually enable you to reach the heights of success you're striving for!

1. *Cultivate humility.*

Arrogant leaders tend to think of humility as weak. That's a false perception. Humility means being realistic about yourself, your ideas, your abilities. It means being honest enough to accept your limitations and admit that you're not perfect. You acknowledge that you can—and do—make mistakes.

At its core, humility is about truth. If you want to move forward, you need to be firmly rooted in the truth.

Business experts around the world have embraced this principle. The late C. K. Prahalad, who was a globally respected corporate strategy and management expert, asserted, "Leadership is self-awareness, recognizing your failings, and developing modesty, humility and humanity." Jim Collins, bestselling author of *Good to Great*, puts humility at the core of what he calls "Level Five Leadership." Collins says of humble leaders: "They routinely credit others, external factors, and good luck for their companies' success. But when results are poor, they blame themselves. They also act quietly, calmly, and determinedly—relying on inspired standards, not inspiring charisma, to motivate."

2. *Acknowledge and apologize.*

If your arrogance has resulted in words or actions that have hurt or put down others, you need to openly acknowledge your inappropriate behavior and apologize for it. Failing to do so and simply attempting to "be nice to everybody" looks phony. Few people will believe you, and the rest will wonder what you're up to. Plus, it will be easy for you to slip back into old patterns at the first provocation.

But a public acknowledgement carries with it a commitment to follow through. It gives you a needed impetus to change your behavior. It also gives people a framework in which to understand and react to your change.

You don't necessarily have to say, "I'm sorry" (though there are no more powerful words in the English language). Try such phrases as "That wasn't my intent," or "I didn't realize my actions had that kind of impact; I only want the best for all of us." You—and your co-workers and employees—can then move on.

Saying "I'm sorry" is a stumbling block for many leaders who have been raised in the "no excuses" school. Perhaps the all-time example of this occurs in the great John Ford western *Fort Apache,* where the veteran cavalry officer played by John Wayne blisters a young lieutenant for a mistake and then tells him, "Don't apologize. It's a sign of weakness."

With all respect for John Ford and John Wayne (we both love the movies they made, separately and together), nothing could be further from the truth. Saying "I'm sorry" and playing the victim, asking for pity—sure, that's a sign of weakness. But owning up to mistakes and apologizing for hurting other people for no good reason—that's a sign of strength. Great leaders know the difference and act accordingly.

3. *Be clear about what you are going to change.*

Sustaining a behavioral change is tough. But it's easier if you're clear and specific right at the start about what you're planning to do differently. And don't keep that information to yourself! Let your peers and staff know about your goals.

Being explicit sets the standard for you personally, and gives your co-workers a solid basis for providing feedback. Like it or not, you will need feedback if you are really going to change. Although it may often result in a painful "ouch," you must both *solicit* and *accept* the comments of others. That means not jumping down someone's throat the first time they call you on your arrogant behavior. Or the second time. Or the third.

Instead, thank the person for their input. Don't justify yourself or try to rationalize. Simply accept the feedback and, as Walt Disney said, "Keep moving forward!" If you are consistent, you'll be saying "ouch" less and less as time goes on.

4. *Invite input from others.*

Arrogance is a very close-minded attitude. To change, you'll need to:

- Be open to ideas.

- Let people express their opinions.

- Become more approachable.

- Listen more.

- Talk less.

- Invite other people's contributions.

- Ask questions, and then let the other person talk.

• Put the other person first.

Life isn't all about you, and the best ideas don't all come from you. It's time to get out of your own way, and everyone else's, and open up to what others have to offer.

5. *Empower your people.*

Let go! Stop controlling everything and give your people back their autonomy. Allow them to do the jobs you brought them in to do. Remember, you hired A-players for a reason. They have skills, talents, and experience your company needs. So cut them loose!

This doesn't mean that you never intervene or give advice. But you will need to move from *telling* people how to do their jobs to *coaching* them in their jobs. Telling is dictatorial. Coaching leads and guides people, but doesn't put them in a straitjacket.

And remember, people have their own styles and methods. A person's approach may be different than yours. But that doesn't make either approach better or worse, as long as the job gets done and gets done well. Besides, who wants a bunch of clones in the office? There is strength in diversity; there is power in differences.

So lighten up, loosen up, and empower your people. You'll find you have a lot fewer headaches when you do.

6. *Give credit where credit is due.*

One last piece of incredibly important advice: give credit where it's due. Recognize people's accomplishments. When someone comes up with a brilliant idea, acknowledge it—right then and there in public. Hand out rewards liberally: verbal affirmations, awards, promotions, recognition, and so on.

Step out of the limelight. Let other people take their bows. And be sure to add your own applause.

3

Insecurity—Respecting Yourself (For a Change)

"Sometimes I wonder how I got to be a division head. I honestly feel most of the time like I'm in too deep, and that one day they will find out who I really am and replace me."

—A Leader with Insecurity HeadTrash

Insecurity is the most crippling of all the HeadTrashes, because no other leadership obstacle is so deeply rooted. If, as the expression goes, "you are what you think," then underneath the bravado that many display, insecure people doubt themselves—all the time. Whenever they look in the mirror, literally or figuratively, they see only what they think is lacking. Whenever they have to make a difficult decision, which is often, the first thing they hear in their heads is self-doubt, and the first emotion they feel is anxiety about not being good enough to meet the challenge they face. They have a story about how inadequate they are, and they're working hard to make the rest of us stick to it, whatever the cost.

Here is how *Merriam-Webster* defines insecurity:

insecurity noun the quality or state of being insecure as
    a: a lack of assurance
    b: lack of safety

What makes insecurity such a debilitating obstacle is that the individual suffering from it doesn't have enough self-confidence to battle against it. Spending vast amounts of time mentally diminishing their talents and their place in the world, insecure leaders impede themselves and work against the common good. That makes them a huge problem for anyone who has to work with them.

Standard Office Operating Procedure for the Insecure: Avoid, Delay, Prolong, Dodge

See if this sounds familiar. Be honest.

Your division has grown to the point that top management wants you to start thinking about a succession plan. In the short term, you need to fill two key positions. But the ultimate goal is to have one of these individuals become your successor, while you move on to greater responsibilities. The company is plainly saying, "We have faith in you to grow the business."

Unfortunately for all concerned, this is not how you are

> *Tim Says: Insecure folks probably struggle the most going from manager to leader. Instead of feeling a sense of accomplishment, they fear that they'll become replaceable.*

thinking about it. Your insecurity HeadTrash makes you fear that one, if not both, of the two new hires will somehow leapfrog over you. That is possible, albeit unlikely. But if you don't get your HeadTrash under control, you will gradually make it more and more likely that your own insecurity, not someone else's excellence, will slow you down or marginalize you.

The recruitment process has identified two particularly

impressive candidates for the two positions. One has a brilliant academic record and seven years of background in your area. Another comes with sterling referrals and a unique blend of experience that would bring in a fresh point of view. If you were honest with yourself, you'd admit that the candidates are good fits for the slots you have to fill.

However, you can't be honest with yourself, and you tell yourself that neither candidate quite meets your (you think quite appropriate) standards. You start making up reasons why neither of them would work out: the candidate with long experience in the industry won't bring enough innovation; the candidate with high academic credentials won't fit in with your trendy culture.

You campaign instead for two people with fewer credentials and less experience, telling everyone that these less qualified candidates are a "steal" and have serious growth potential. Imaginary bullets dodged, you go back to your "safe" existence. Unfortunately, you've hurt the business and yourself by not bringing in the best talent. The less talented people you have insisted on hiring will be less able to grow the business. And you will wind up staying longer than you need to at your current level, if indeed you ever do earn that promotion to greater responsibilities.

What Insecure People Say to Themselves

Insecurity, like other forms of HeadTrash, is so difficult to overcome because it takes self-awareness and honesty simply to recognize it. The added challenge with insecurity is that even if you are self-aware enough to 'fess up and face the internal music, you probably won't have enough courage to do what needs to be done, because, well, you're too insecure. It's a vicious cycle.

Insecure people tend to have very noisy brains, filled with negative imagery and self-talk that may date back to their child-hood. This "glass-is-half-empty" feedback loop simply reinforces their doubts and fears. Some feel like victims with the deck stacked against them, and each perceived slight affirms their point of view. An e-mail that someone else might read as neutral is riddled with threats for the insecure person. An assignment that presents a challenge but contains big opportunities for growth looks like a time bomb, a setup for failure.

FBI: Five Fatal Behaviors of the Insecure

Insecure leaders are dangerous to themselves and to their organizations because this HeadTrash manifests itself in a number of negative behaviors.

FBI I: CONFIRMING THEIR BAD SELVES

Insecure people begin with a negative belief about themselves, a condition psychologists call the impostor syndrome. Coined by clinical psychologists Pauline Clance and Suzanne Imes in their 1978 book, *The Impostor Phenomenon Among High Achieving Women: Dynamics and Therapeutic Intervention*, the phrase refers to people who remain convinced that they're frauds, regardless of the success they've achieved. They write off their achievements as luck, timing, or deception.

Fearful of being found out for the inadequate posers they think they are, people with impostor syndrome often "prove" their unworthiness with self-sabotaging conduct. One example is turning in a report late, using procrastination as way of avoiding the bad news they expect to hear. We see procrastination and perfectionism as opposite sides of the same coin—both feed the insecure person's underlying belief that they and their work are never good enough.

Other examples might be lashing out after a perceived slight, or an overreaction to an alleged offense. The insecure person is always prone to feeling, and then somehow confirming, a negative self-judgment—"See, I really am a failure."

FBI II: PREVENTING THE PEOPLE AROUND YOU FROM GROWING

One of the best ways to spot an insecure leader is to look at their subordinates. If the team is underdeveloped, stifled, and feeling boxed in, chances are the boss doesn't have the self-confidence to advocate for their growth. In fact, many managers want to keep their people right where they are, because it's safer to maintain the status quo.

FBI III: GRABBING CREDIT

Worried that he or she is not getting their due, and needing props to boost their weak self-esteem, the insecure leader rarely shares credit with the team. Whatever is achieved is ultimately for her greater glory, and she is quite vocal about replaying how the great idea or big sale came to be, casting herself in the starring role. There is never enough air to fill the balloon, because the balloon has a hole in it. What insecure people don't realize is *that true leaders share credit, offering praise and perks as a way to elevate and motivate the people around them.* They fail to recognize that when their team succeeds, everyone gets rewarded, including them.

FBI IV: DEFENSIVENESS

It's hard to hear constructive criticism because you're so afraid that others might confirm your most deeply held negative beliefs about yourself. Instead of growing from feedback, you lash out to defend yourself because the message hit home. The feedback may be a growth opportunity, but you're not interested. The insecure person doesn't realize that all feedback is a gift, if you use it the right way.

FBI V: TEARING OTHERS DOWN TO BUILD YOURSELF UP

It's never a good idea to make your clients feel dumb. And it's not much smarter to belittle a colleague. Yet extremely insecure people often think nothing of publicly crushing anyone who disagrees with them, winning the battle but losing the war. They sacrifice accounts, upset team relations, and kill future career options by making enemies they don't even know they have.

BEHIND THE SCENES WITH TISH & TIM:
INSECURITY ANECDOTE I—VARIATIONS ON A THEME

We've already mentioned that each HeadTrash can take different forms. Whenever we talk about insecurity Tim brings up a genius-level woman executive in the retail industry, a brilliant strategist with super-duper high energy and a wonderful ability to connect people in productive ways. She really knew how to build strong teams and an inspiring work environment. But she never owned her abilities. She was a giant ball of insecurity, and always felt that she was about to be exposed as a fraud. And it was all driven by her lack of self-confidence.

The empirical data was just the opposite. Everyone thought she was brilliant. Her boss loved her, her team loved working with and for her. Everyone respected her because of her commitment to their development. But she never felt she could measure up. This insecurity led her to leave the company because she never felt she could meet the expectations of the job. Ironically, the bigger loss was for the company—it lost a highly talented professional with tons of potential because no one in higher management recognized and addressed the signs of her insecurity HeadTrash.

Tish just as quickly brings up the fact that it's usually the most insecure people who talk the most about their achievements, trying to convince themselves of how great they are. But when they look in the mirror, they don't believe the positive things they are saying about themselves. And they brag and boast, because they believe others don't believe in them, either.

It is ironic that insecure people can present themselves in completely opposite ways, self-loathing or self-promoting. But in either case the underlying HeadTrash is the same.

Caution versus Doubt:
The Difference Seems Subtle; the Results Are Glaring!

Ah yes, we can hear you, Mr. or Ms. Insecure, hoping to look responsible. "I avoid risk because I want to do the right thing for the organization." That point of view is admirable. In any big decision, there's too much at stake for a snap judgment.

But there are a number of differences between a cautious leader and an insecure one. To the untrained eye, they might look the same, because putting off a decision can seem like an insecure act. But caution and insecurity are vastly different. And the proof is how very different the results are.

An Insecurity Checklist and Comparison

Which column sounds more like you?

A CAUTIOUS LEADER...	AN INSECURE LEADER...
Doesn't commit in either direction at the beginning of the decision process.	Rushes to tell you why the project can't be done.
Gathers more data by asking probing questions before offering an opinion.	Offers answers without asking the probing questions.
Steps to the front of the line and stays in the game until it's done.	Talks a good game, but is gone baby gone when things get tough!
Inspires participation by seeking help and input from the team.	Has a hard time allowing anyone else into the process.
Is quick to share credit.	Is quick to grab credit.
Wants to find someone she can share the load with.	Can't find anyone good enough to help carry the ball.

HeadTrash Alert! A Quick Quiz on Insecurity

Please rate yourself on the following statements by placing a checkmark in the appropriate column:

	Never	Sometimes	Often	Always
When I am assigned a new project, my first thought is, "I can't do this."				
I have thought to myself, "I was assigned this task because my boss is testing me."				
I obsess over deadlines and believe most are too severe for me to meet.				
I hate presenting at executive meetings.				
I am reluctant to hire people who have better credentials than I do because I fear I'm training my replacement.				
I find it very difficult to be open to feedback.				
I often put off projects in the hopes they will just go away.				

Tim Says: When we work with a person who is insecure, our first goal is to help them to get more comfortable in their own skin. Eventually you can get them to start to see their real self-worth, but that doesn't happen right away.

Tish Says: That's true, but I think you have to help them 'define' their skin, help them recognize and accept the pros and the cons. Always focus on the positive, without sugar coating it.

How Do Insecure People Become Leaders?
Sheer Determination and Resilience

How do insecure people become leaders in the first place? Why doesn't their insecurity keep them from rising in an organization? Our experience has been that many insecure people counterbalance their self-perceived lack of worth or potential by working harder than anyone else. The determination and resilience of the insecure person actually stem from the fear of being uncovered as being incapable. Ironically, this hard work earns them points with superiors and managers who end up promoting them. They earn titles, kudos, and rewards, but the underlying insecurity remains. Now they have more responsibility, more people to manage and more critical decisions to make—all things that will heighten their insecurity.

Re: Insecurity
From the desk of: Chris Saridakis, CEO of GSI Commerce

Chris Saridakis, CEO of GSI Commerce, a leading provider of services that fuel e-commerce, multichannel retailing, and interactive marketing internationally, has this to say about insecurity:

"When I recruit for my own management team, who are pretty seasoned professionals, the one thing I look for, that element that makes or breaks my decision, is that they are not insecure leaders. And by 'insecure' I mean not only those who appear insecure in an interview, but also those who show fake confidence by continually talking about how accomplished they are."

Of all the HeadTrashes, Saridakis considers a lack of self-confidence among the worst for causing company-wide damage. "Insecurity," he said, "can be very debilitating to an organization. People don't want to follow someone who is insecure."

Insecurity can show up in any activity a leader engages in, from the daily and mundane to the critical and monumental. "Meetings become bigger. E-mail lists start with one or two people, and suddenly they've copied nine or ten people on it because they're not confident that one person will get it done. You see behaviors that slow down an organization, and decision making that doesn't get done in a way that more confident and commanding leaders will just do."

And when the moment arrives to actually make a big commitment, to take that buzzer-beater shot, the self-doubter usually passes the ball.

"The insecure leader is probably the one who just can't make a decision, who manages decision making through consensus, and won't take risks." And that, says Saridakis, puts the people above these leaders—those at the top of the company—in a state of concern and doubt.

"If you have nine or ten direct reports, and one of the direct reports has too much insecurity, whether it's about their position in the organization or their own abilities, you are always going to worry about that person. You're always going to worry about that person's team."

But the problem isn't restricted to the doubtful leader. Insecurity, according Saridakis, is often built into company cultures. "Some companies have a mentality of 'We can't fail. We're too big to fail.' If they're a pharmaceutical company, they've got to have the perfect compound. Or whatever it may be. It's ridiculous. I don't think large corporations budget failure productively.

"They may have twenty, thirty, sixty years of success. So they hire managers and leaders who will confidently show that, yes, we'll keep the train on the tracks. But when it comes to a decision that may be out of their comfort zone, that may be more entrepreneurial or new, they're not to going to make that decision on their own. And that's where the insecurity kicks in. Then they question if they are even qualified to do this. So they ask ten people, and those ten people ask twenty people. All of a sudden, it slows the organization down."

What is the antidote to insecurity? Well, it's a process. As Saridakis says, it begins with letting leaders know that they can grow, and that it's okay to fail forward. That is, you should realize that mistakes are inevitable, that they are opportunities to learn and part of doing anything worthwhile, especially anything innovative, and that the only bad mistakes are those a person makes without conscious awareness.

"You need those moments where you can give someone the key and say, 'Look, I know this may not be comfortable for you, but try it out. Take the biggest risk you can. We're going to win or lose on this, and if we lose, no problem. But if we win, you'll have more confidence than you ever did.'"

Recommendations for Overcoming the HeadTrash of Insecurity

MOVING FROM SELF-DOUBT TO SELF-CONFIDENCE

As remarkable as this may sound, insecure people usually don't see how self-destructive they really are. While most are aware of their insecurities, they view the behavior that accompanies it as justifiable self-defense, workplace jujitsu that keeps them from being "discovered" for the frauds they think they are. They're the first people to undervalue their achievements with phrases like, "Well, I was lucky," or "Yes, but anyone could have done that."

How do you get out of this morass of insecurity? You must take an accurate self-inventory in order to see yourself as you really are. Ask yourself, "What empirical evidence do I have that I am not good enough?" Make a list of your strengths, because you have them. At the same time list your weaknesses, because you have them, too. Seek the feedback of others through a 360-degree evaluation and/or ask your manager and colleagues for input. Insecure leaders are often so caught up in their own "stuff" that they require input from others to provide a reality check. Once you get comfortable with who you really are, you'll be able to see how to grow your strengths and compensate for your areas of weakness. And then you can build a team that will complement you so that teamwork becomes a way to success, and not the enemy.

The first step to seeing yourself for who you really are is reversing and improving the basic conversations you have with yourself. You must turn self-trashing into self-respecting, based on the facts and not the drama. Say things like:

- "I can do this!"

- "I'm not a victim."

- "Maybe I'm overreacting."

- "I like a good challenge."

Repeat and repeat and repeat to yourself the positive thoughts and feelings you want to experience, based on your actual accomplishments to date. Reach out to a trusted colleague or coach, if you have one, to remind yourself of your recent accomplishments and victories. This should help you to reprogram the way you think about yourself, so that you can begin to believe the positive truth. Of course, this reprogramming has to work against decades of emotional self-denigration.

Here are five habits to practice as you reprogram inaccurate self-trashing into appropriate self-respecting:

1. *Truly embrace compliments and value your worth.*
   Instead of leaping to devalue yourself, grab the opportunity to pat yourself on the back after any success. It may be as simple as allowing yourself to accept a compliment without diminishing the praise. Then fan that spark of positive feedback into a small fire that you learn how to feed. If you can't do it for yourself, find a career coach or counselor who can help you. Your life and career are too important to be held hostage.

2. *Feed your noisy brain with the right stuff.*
   We noted that insecure people have noisy brains, reminding themselves constantly of how lacking they are. Your goal is to change the self-talk, to make it more realistic. When you make a mistake, don't say, "I've always screwed up before, and

I've screwed up again." Say, "Mistakes are part of life. I will learn from this and try not to make that mistake again."

3. *Stop comparing.*

Few activities are as self-destructive as measuring yourself against others. "I may have generated a 5 percent boost in incremental sales, but she generated 8 percent and her brand has better research scores. What am I doing wrong?" That is not the question to ask. Instead ask, "What I am doing right, and how can I improve?" Or tell yourself and your team, "If they can boost 8 percent, then our goal should be 10 percent."

4. *Accentuate the positive.*

Self-confidence literally means having faith in yourself. For the insecure person, that can be challenging, but challenge is a key part of growth. Your job is to test your perceptions of yourself, to lose your sense of victimhood, and see who you really are. Performance reviews often present the opportunity to highlight your inner winner, forcing you to make a rational business case for why you are worthy of a promotion. So ask for it. Embrace it! Build your case with confidence, and then let the reality of who you are change your point of view. In truth, you have probably already earned the respect and endorsement of your superiors. And the only person you really needed to persuade is you.

5. *Do it for the team.*

Not willing to see how you're crippling yourself? Then perhaps you'll be willing to admit how your insecurity is wounding others. Maybe you'll be inspired to work on yourself for the greater good. Losing revenue, sidelining talented people, and jeopardizing business growth are all potential outcomes of poor self-worth. Because of the affect on others, who you are and how you behave are actually bigger than you. And since there is so much at risk, the time to begin changing really is now.

Understand that this process of reprogramming and reinforcement will take time, so be patient with yourself. Major change in how you view yourself will not happen overnight, but it must start with *you* for it to take flight

BEHIND THE SCENES WITH TISH & TIM: INSECURITY ANECDOTE II —THE MAN IN THE MIRROR

One of our more challenging clients was the CEO of a European-based digital technology company who was tasked with establishing a U.S. presence. Despite his career success in Europe, he was convinced that he was going to have a very challenging time succeeding in the United States. Using many of the tactics described in this chapter, we provided this leader with a regular reality check about his performance. Through the use of a 360-degree appraisal and by asking simple and direct questions such as "What feedback are you getting from the board about your performance?" (Answer: "Exceeding expectations") or "What are you hearing from your colleagues?" (Answers: "Great team player. Great big-picture thinker. Tremendous asset to the company. Develops his people extremely well"), we were able show this leader empirical evidence of his outstanding performance.

Seeing the positive feedback in the black and white of the 360 report and hearing us pose questions that he was not asking himself because of his lack of positive self-belief, the executive became able to accept what others actually saw in him. Over time his confidence grew stronger and stronger. He was able to build and scale the business thanks to feeling secure enough to hire top talent, trusting in his own abilities to communicate and be transparent with his team on the challenges that lie ahead, and learning to integrate his own style with the business culture of the United States.

4

Control— Letting Go and Learning to Delegate and Collaborate

"A few of my people accuse me of being a control freak. But I know what's best for the business. Honestly, if I didn't step in, I wonder if they'd know what to do half the time."
—A Leader with Control HeadTrash

Whether you own the company or are a senior member of the executive team, it's easy to think that you're not only the captain of the ship, you're also the propeller and the rudder. Doesn't your track record of success prove the point? Without your hands-on management style, the business could never have become what it is today.

If you're honest with yourself, however, you suspect that you might have some control issues. You've probably caught wind of the whispering at meetings, and seen some of your best employees bristle at your micromanagement style. Now you find yourself more overloaded than ever, thinking that no one appreciates the stress you're under.

You wonder if it's all worth it.

The answer is, yes, it is all worth it, but you are going to have to let go. Being a great leader means empowering your people, giving them the control to make decisions and manage their teams and their own success.

First let's answer the question, "What is **control**?" *Merriam-Webster* defines the noun "control" in this way:

> *1: a:* an act or instance of controlling; also: power or authority to guide or manage
>
> *b:* skill in the use of a tool, instrument, technique, or artistic medium
>
> *c:* the regulation of economic activity especially by government directive—usually used in plural <price controls>
>
> *d:* the ability of a baseball pitcher to control the location of a pitch within the strike zone
>
> *2:* restraint, reserve
>
> *3:* one that controls …

Those things don't sound horrible, do they? They may or may not be, because control isn't necessarily bad. There are degrees of control and appropriate times to apply it.

For instance, teachers need to have control of their classrooms, otherwise there would be chaos and nothing would get accomplished. Or say your child is about to run into the street. You need to have established enough parental control that your "Stop!" keeps your child from running into harm's way.

In other words, there is appropriate, productive control, and there is inappropriate, counterproductive control. It's not always as simple as looking at the bottom line to spot the difference. But you need to know that getting productive control means giving up counterproductive control.

Good Control versus Bad Control

Control is one of the easiest forms of HeadTrash for a leader to self-justify. After all, you've had your finger on the pulse of your company for a long time!

When you're in the entrepreneurial phase of a company or division, and you're growing the business, it's all bootstraps and long hours. As a leader, you're involved in every aspect of the budding enterprise, because you and a handful of others are doing the work of twenty people.

Then, all of a sudden, there are twenty people working for your business, while you modify your controls and processes only slightly to suit the larger scale. Then, lo and behold, you hit a new threshold. Suddenly, there are fifty employees, while you as the leader remain entrenched in your original mode of controlling every detail. That is how you got here. Even though it's incredibly stressful, you think it's still working.

In time, however, your smothering control will frustrate good people. The lack of autonomy will motivate your stars to leave, typically to help grow another company (maybe your competitor) in ways you did not allow when they were working for you.

Successful leaders recognize achievement and reward it by expanding responsibilities. They enhance their ability to manage a growing enterprise by sharing control and encouraging everyone to reach their full potential. Giving your best players the space and autonomy to be outstanding enables you to hold onto them longer. It builds a powerful team *from within,* developing what baseball teams call the "farm club." And it attracts the best talent from outside your business. Great leaders make their organizations talent magnets by distributing leadership and decision-making responsibilities, rather than hoarding them.

People who suffer from control HeadTrash believe that keeping a tight rein on every aspect of the business will ensure its long-term success. That's a fallacy. As a business grows, it becomes impossible for one person to run everything. It's impractical, it's unsustainable, and it's certainly no way to scale your business for growth.

Making matters even worse, excessive control triggers other types of HeadTrash (insecurity, paranoia, fear) in your colleagues. With limited opportunity to express their talents, employees often start to doubt themselves. "Why doesn't my boss think I can handle this? There must be something I'm not doing right." Beware of the negative effect your need for control has on others.

> *Tim Says: Complete control is an illusion. The only things you can attempt to control are your thoughts and feelings.*

> *Tish Says: Don't confuse operational controls with an individual that is controlling. Operational controls are critical in the effective running of a business while a controlling manager can be very detrimental to a company's success.*

Many leaders don't understand the difference between being decisive and being controlling. Sometimes you have to step in and make the call, because you have knowledge or experience that others don't. That's exerting positive control. If you know that something is going in the wrong direction, it's irresponsible to allow it to continue for long. The trick is understanding the difference between responsible involvement and decision making on the one hand, and micromanaging every detail on the other.

Symptoms of Control HeadTrash in the Office

- Your superstars leave.

- You can feel the frustration.

- Disappointment is in the air.

- You develop robotic, compliant employees.

- People stop thinking. They wait to be told what to do.

- Creativity is smothered. People ask themselves, "Why bother?"

- Communication runs one-way—from boss to employees.

Types of Controlling Personalities

- **SUBTLE CONTROL FREAK**

    Subtle control freaks tend to be passive-aggressive. They look like they're sharing responsibility, doling out authority and opportunity. But then they take it back, if they ever gave it at all, in ways that look positive.

    For example, we once worked with the CEO of a growing company who decided to bring in someone to run the sales team. The CEO made an excellent hire. Preparing to roll out his first initiative, the new sales leader ran it by the CEO as a courtesy. But due to his inability to let go and his need to control the situation, the CEO dictated exactly how the initiative should be executed, right down to the smallest detail. The CEO had given the illusion of empowerment, but for all intents and purposes he was still running the sales team—and everything else.

This form of control is especially insidious for the leader because subtle control is difficult to detect and oftentimes goes unnoticed. In the scenario we've just outlined, it was not until the new head of sales quit that the CEO accepted the need to be less controlling.

Monday 9:00 a.m.

"This is your project. I have faith that you can handle it. Let me know if you need anything."

Monday 11:00 a.m.

"So, how's the project coming? I was thinking, if you're going to have a meeting on this, I'd like to sit in on it."

Tim had a client who was so proud of the controls she had put in place that, even when the company scaled and the controls needed to change to meet client needs, she simply could not let go. She ultimately hurt both the company and her own credibility. Controls that were originally quite legitimate and necessary had become a means to control others.

• **MICROMANAGER CONTROL FREAK**

The micromanager is overt, pedantic, and crushes people in excruciating minutiae. "This is the way I want you to do this. Now go do it," such managers say, articulating their expectations step by step.

They believe people need to be told exactly what to do, because left to their own devices they'd be lazy and unproductive. This is the viewpoint of an authoritarian parent who dictates to children without ever listening to them. That makes the micromanagers feel powerful, while everyone else feels belittled.

• **HOARDER-OF-KNOWLEDGE CONTROL FREAK**

The hoarder of knowledge saws off power and information. Only *she* knows all the details, which she parcels out in increments to different players. Each employee has just a piece of the puzzle, thereby creating narrow experts. But since the hoarder is the only one who has all the facts, she believes she's assured her authority.

At times, the hoarder will give the same or a similar assignment to several people. They all think they're in charge of the project. But the hoarder, controlling information like a stubborn faucet, turns on a weak stream for some and a fuller stream for others. It can be a means of setting people against each other and sitting back while the underlings sort it out, or duke it out, as the case may be.

• MANAGEMENT SYSTEM CONTROL FREAK

In our experience as consultants, we have frequently seen management systems like Six Sigma, ISO 9000, and CRM software—all potentially valuable, and in some cases necessary, tools—used to enforce behavior and instill fear and compliance.

Control-freak bosses love management systems. In the name of efficiency, they employ them to eliminate autonomy, causing their staff to shy away from thinking creatively and taking appropriate risks.

"We'll just wait for the boss to tell us what to do," say the overmanaged employees, their resentment building. And, in the same way that insecurity can be passed down from an unsure leader to a now doubting employee, control trauma also filters down. Like a domino, it goes from leader and senior management to middle management and down through the ranks, until the kid in the mailroom won't sort the envelopes until told.

Tim Says: A company's culture is the behavior of its leaders. HeadTrash like control can become institutionalized.

A Control Checklist and Comparison

Which column sounds more like you?

A CONTROLLING LEADER...	AN EMPOWERING LEADER...
Holds people back.	Urges people on.
Creates compliant employees.	Creates committed employees.
Dominates.	Influences.
Makes employees fearful.	Creates a safe environment.
Oversees *everything*.	Delegates responsibility.
Can make the company implode.	Helps the company flourish.
Stifles new thinking.	Fuels innovation.
Keeps people guessing.	Is open and clear on big issues.

HeadTrash Alert! A Quick Quiz on Control

Please rate yourself on the following statements by placing a checkmark in the appropriate column:

	Never	Sometimes	Often	Always
I need to be in every single meeting to ensure that the right decisions are made.				
People are uncomfortable coming to me for further direction on a project.				
I struggle allowing my employees to make decisions without my approval.				
My work environment is eerily quiet.				
I spend too much of my time correcting others' work.				
When I delegate a project, I expect I will be part of its execution.				
I find myself looking for status updates prior to the agreed project milestones.				
I struggle with fully delegating highly visible assignments to someone else.				

If you checked "often" or "always" three or more times, you probably suffer from control HeadTrash.

" To save time, just let me know if there is anything in here I did <u>right</u>."

Juggling China versus Juggling Tupperware

When you have a lot of things on your plate, you have to prioritize. Here's an approach to beginning the process we call the china versus Tupperware test. Some issues are Tupperware challenges. If you juggle Tupperware and it falls, you or someone else can still pick it up and keep moving. It may be a little dented, or it may survive the fall without any damage. Either way, you haven't lost anything.

Under these guidelines, that assignment can be delegated.

Conversely, if you juggle good china and you drop it, it shatters. Those initiatives you probably want to handle yourself, or delegate to one of your superstars.

Control freaks believe that *everything* is fine china, *everything* is urgent and essential and can only be handled by one person. (Guess who?)

When every project and decision is a here-and-now crisis, long-term thinking vanishes. Without clear direction and a plan, you and your staff are either all over the place or stuck in crisis mode. You fail, and the company falters.

If there are fifteen things on your to-do list, surely not all of them rise to china-level concern. Decide which tasks you truly can delegate. Then call those Tupperware, and act accordingly.

> *Tish Says: Do you find yourself spending fourteen to sixteen hours a day on things that don't move the company forward? Don't mistake activity for productivity.*

Good Leaders Make It Look Easy

Good leaders delegate. They build strong teams by hiring talented people, then step away and allow them to flourish.

Tim has a client who, on the face of it, doesn't look like a great leader because he's so relaxed and he delegates so much. He's so laissez-faire, his leadership style is almost invisible. But he has a rockin' company, because he sets a clear framework and then lets people do their thing.

Re: Control
From the desks of Marta Martinez, AOL Head of Sales Strategies and Operations, and Chris Saridakis, CEO GSI Commerce

If there are two people you'd want to have controlling your business, it would be Marta Martinez and Chris Saridakis. Martinez's high-level executive positions in the digital media industry include serving as CMO at online media buying agency MediaMath during triple-digit growth years, from 2007 to 2011. Saridakis, as we mentioned earlier, is CEO at e-commerce services provider GSI Commerce. Both of these respected leaders are quick to say that the impulse to control everything, understandable though it may be, is counterproductive.

"Everyone falls into the trap of taking too much control of a situation," says Saridakis. "We're all guilty of it. Everyone has some form of HeadTrash around control, because most successful people grew up as doers. Most leaders are not born running companies."

Martinez agrees, saying that the ability to manage and lead without interfering in every action is job number one for a leader. "An executive should be setting direction and making sure the team stays on focus."

Which begs the question: why are some leaders so controlling? "Because they are very smart, and they know better than everyone else," says Martinez with a wink. "If you know better than everyone else, then you want to make sure things are done exactly how you want them done."

Control HeadTrash can indeed reflect an underlying problem of arrogance. But it can also reflect insecurity. Saridakis says the control urge could be the doubt you're feeling "when you don't believe you have the right team in place. So what you may do instead of making tougher decisions to replace that team, is to take more control and do more things yourself. To cover up the fact that maybe you haven't hired that well."

Unfortunately, leaders who continually do for others cause their people to second guess themselves. And instead of taking the initiative, Martinez says, doubtful employees learn to wait around for the chief to tip his or her hand on how they want something done. "Employees' fear of doing something wrong becomes a bottleneck. It doesn't allow the company to grow. Speed to market gets reduced. Control has a direct relationship to speed to market." "It can slow down an entire organization," Saridakis adds.

The best solution, according to Martinez, is to encourage everyone in the organization to share common values and goals. That way, people in different parts of the company are motivated to row in the same direction. "You can establish cultural boundaries, such as setting clear expectations around what is considered unacceptable behavior (e.g., giving a date for completion of a project, but then asking for multiple updates each day) to help you, so that you don't have to be so controlling. Strong vision and strategy, with a supporting culture, can you help overcome the need for control."

One of Saridakis's primary yardsticks for the success of a company and the person leading it is the ability to share control. "Do you hire great people who can be empowered to make decisions and do things with very little involvement? That's another form of how you evaluate a leader."

Recommendations for Overcoming the HeadTrash of Control

FROM CONTROL TO TRUST AND INSPIRATION

One of the most surprising insights for overly controlling leaders is that their desire to rule every person and detail in their businesses often grows out of arrogance, insecurity, or fear. For many, it's a stunning revelation because they're so convinced their behavior is positive and well meaning, they can't see that the inspiration for their style is often negative. But if you're guilty of trying to exercise too much control, and can stop and look behind what's driving your actions, you'll often find fear or arrogance.

Fear that something, anything, will go horribly wrong without your being able to manage it. Fear that you'll be exposed as anything less than the minor deity you think your company needs. Fear that perhaps you made the wrong hires along the way.

Arrogance that says you and you and alone know what's best, despite how the people around you have proven themselves. Arrogance that says you must be the recipient of all significant company kudos. Arrogance that says your competition could never hire away one of your key people, no matter what the circumstances.

It's not surprising that many successful leaders confuse fear or willful pride with being proactive or confident. As we said earlier, there's nothing wrong with being decisive and taking action when you know what's best for your business. And confidence is hardly a bad character trait. It's often the key factor in helping take a company or a division from zero to sixty miles-per-hour in no time flat.

But here you are with a large and growing company that is still too you-centric. How do you fix it? You can't remedy what you can't identify or are unwilling to admit. So step back and search for signs that you have control HeadTrash. Assuming you do, you'll see the signs if you look.

1. *Look at yourself.*

For example, look at some of the work your team is doing and ask, "Do I really need to be involved? Does this really require so much of my attention?" Before you dive into a new time-consuming initiative, see if you can't delegate it instead.

And if you're sincere about wanting to change, ask yourself perhaps the hardest question of all: "Am I getting in the way?"

2. *Look at your people.*

Employees who have been under the thumb of a heavy-handed leader speak volumes—with their body language or their silence. For instance, if you're the only one talking during meetings, guess who is dominating the moment yet again. If you feel like you have been acting on projects alone, ask yourself if that is really the case. When you give direction, do you detect disappointment, defeat, or frustration on the faces and in the voices of your team members? If so, you're probably co-opting an assignment and squashing someone's passion, instead of offering legitimate coaching or management. Have your people stopped offering their ideas, become less creative, or grown less engaged in their work? Such behaviors are signs of people who work for an overly controlling leader—compliant employees, but not engaged ones.

3. *Talk it before you walk it. Praise, ask, or offer versus just do.*

Overly controlling leaders assume they're hosting every party. Instead, behave like a guest—the results will surprise you.

When you're curious about what an employee is doing, lead with a compliment rather than an interrogation. A little praise goes a long way before asking, "How did you come to that decision?" And if you really think you should be involved (be honest, now) try saying, "The team appears very engaged. If there's anything I can help you with, please know I'm here." Or offer to take a small role, allowing your employees to retain ownership and move ahead without looking for constant approval. It's the way great companies cultivate future leaders.

4. *Signs of progress will appear, often quickly.*

People talk, but not just about the negatives. Good news spreads, too, especially when it's about a change in a leader's behavior. Once people hear and believe that you're loosening the reins, you'll note others *asking* you for your input and opinion, often those who might not have done so before. They'll welcome your feedback and thoughts. You will be included in more meetings (informally and formally). Folks will come to you more often looking for ideas. In short, they'll make you part of the team, and you'll no longer have to force your way in.

5. *Keep your management/measurement tools, but involve other people.*

You don't need to scrap what's working, and good operational tools enable you to keep score and improve efficiency. But the less robotic you make the process, the more your company will flourish. Share what you're seeing on your dashboard, invite suggestions for improving your operational controls, and delegate responsibility for as much of the process of collecting and evaluating the data as possible. The more your people feel they have ownership of key operational measures, the harder and more creatively they will strive to meet and exceed them.

6. *Remedies in Action: Let go, and stop before you start.*

- *"Let things go."* Letting things go is a concept most leaders can't fathom, especially if things aren't moving along as they'd like. But purposely allowing some things to fail generates situations where others can be held accountable. It also creates an opening to talk to a team that may actually welcome guidance, instead just inserting yourself. Obviously, you will need to calculate the risk of allowing a failure, but some failures are more serious than others.

- *Nipping your control impulse in midstream.* You are who you are, and you'll be prone to behave the way you have for years. Conversely, nothing is more powerful than a leader who says openly, "Oops, there I go again." Admitting to your team that you may be "over-eager to help," and then removing yourself from the process publicly, is more effective than repeating what others may view as your megalomania. It demonstrates the new you for all who witness it.

All of these suggestions boil down to two things: the controlling person must develop awareness of the trait, and then he or she must have the willingness to do something about it. Start with those, and the rest will be a lot easier.

BEHIND THE SCENES WITH TISH & TIM:
CONTROL ANECDOTE—ONE SIZE DOES NOT FIT ALL

We were once hired to coach a high-potential, first-time manager for a family-owned fitness equipment company who was having great difficulties transitioning from being a great individual performer to leading others. He had never received formal training in the art of managing others, and his model for leadership was his former supervisor who was, to put it mildly, a micromanaging control freak. Knowing no better, the first-time manager simply imitated the only model he had: close supervision, multiple follow-up meetings during projects, and what his direct reports called the "infamous red pen." No matter what a subordinate handed him, this manager ripped it to shreds by correcting it using a red pen. Within six months, team members were becoming disengaged with their work. Superstars on the team felt stifled, and all the team members began to ask, "Why should we work so hard on deliverables? He's just going to rip it to shreds anyway!"

Through a 360-degree feedback process, the manager came to realize just how damaging his behavior was to team effectiveness and morale. Over time, he learned that the style modeled for him by his former supervisor was not the only game in town. Through extensive coaching in how to vary his style based on the needs of the employee and the situation, the manager became far less controlling. For example, by using the principles of situational leadership developed by Paul Hersey, he was able to flex his style based on his employees' ability and willingness to perform certain tasks. He came to realize that "one size does not fit all" when it comes to leadership behaviors. As a result, his team became much more effective and productive.

5

Anger—
No Longer Crossing the Line

"Sometimes my people do things that make me so furious, I feel like I have to make a point and raise my voice. I think I'm just being forceful. But occasionally I see the fear in people's eyes, and I wonder if I'm going overboard."
—A Leader with Anger HeadTrash

It was an important meeting, an off-site session where your senior teams were scheduled to present strategies the company desperately needed to generate new revenue. The desired outcome of this gathering was a program to cultivate new markets that would motivate and engage everyone in the company.

When you arrived at 8:00 a.m., you were all smiles and sunshine.

But no more than an hour into the meeting, your stomach began churning. It was clear the plan the first team was presenting, the one they had been working on for months, was weak. Actually, you thought it was pathetic. Some of the ideas sounded like retreads of things you'd already dismissed—hadn't you? To clarify that, you asked a few questions. And then it happened.

One of their responses didn't sit right with you, and in the middle of your reply you snapped. Within seconds, you were shouting and pounding the table, launching a tirade at the presenters, who stared at you pale and shaken, not sure what hit them.

And if you're honest with yourself, you're not quite sure what hit you, either, even though you felt justified at the time.

Which begs the question, why do some leaders get so angry, and feel justified in displaying it publicly? To understand the dynamics, let's ask *Merriam-Webster*, "What is anger?"

anger *noun*
   1: a strong feeling of displeasure and usually of antagonism
   2: rage

Ah, *Merriam-Webster* does it again, because this definition not only describes anger, but also provides important clues for what makes anger either productive or corrosive.

As a leader, you must express your observations, positive and negative, to your staff, and sometimes you have to convey a "strong feeling of displeasure." However, when the subject of your displeasure senses "antagonism," or worse, "rage," your anger has gone off the rails. A leader whose subordinates tag him as hostile does the company more harm than good. He's also hurting himself. To quote Mark Twain, "Anger is an acid that can do more harm to the vessel in which it is stored than to anything on which it is poured."

Appropriate Anger versus Destructive Rage

The best leaders are actually teachers and motivators, catalysts and communicators. It's the leader's job, according to most management theories, to hire good people, give them the tools and guidance they need, and then get the heck out of their way. But good leaders know that there are times when you have to do more than be supportive. Sometimes you need to express your "displeasure" in ways that make the point and generate change. Sometimes a coach has to lay into a team for its poor performance.

The ability to do that is a talent every great leader needs to master. Expressed skillfully, justified anger can have a powerful positive effect. Expressed unskillfully, however, anger, whether fundamentally justified or unjustified, spreads fear and mistrust throughout a company like nerve gas. The effect is damaging and lingering, causing the staff to stop giving their best and sharing their honest opinions. When people feel their jobs are at stake, they take the path of least resistance in order to avoid the wrath from above. And the most capable people take jobs at other companies as soon as possible.

Problems with anger occur when an angry message turns antagonistic. It then becomes very difficult for the recipient to avoid feeling emotionally battered, which is not a good foundation for productive change. Even if you are righteously angry about someone's personal mistake on the job, you must also convey that you want to help the staff member to learn from the mistake and that you have confidence he or she can do so. If you've ever heard someone reminisce fondly about a coach or a teacher who was especially demanding and tough, you will almost certainly hear some variation on the following: "We all knew he/she had our best interests at heart."

If you have justifiably lost faith in an employee because of failure to learn from a series of mistakes, despite appropriate guidance on your or other managers' parts, expressing anger toward that person is really a waste of energy. It is past time to separate the employee from your business so that both of you can move on. By the same token, if you have simply raged at past mistakes as you are raging at the latest one, and have not offered appropriate coaching and support for improved performance, you need to look at your own leadership mistakes before you start firing people and hiring replacements.

Symptoms of an Angry Leader

- A climate of fear influences everything and everyone at the office.

- Employees avoid taking risks, and rarely reach their potential.

- Innovation and creativity are smothered.

- A "CYA" (Cover Your Assets) culture becomes the norm.

- Instead of doing what's best for the business, employees play "Please the Beast." To reduce the pain, they say whatever they think the boss wants to hear.

Four Primary Types of Anger

• DEMONSTRATIVE HOSTILITY

Everyone knows this kind of anger, because there's no mistaking it. The person in charge is fuming, raging out loud because she wants everyone to know she is Ticked Off! She Who Must Be Obeyed never hesitates to show that she is beyond dismayed, engaging in diatribes instead of dialogues that might actually produce a solution. Raging leaders create a workplace of dispirited, disengaged employees. When the leader has a demonstratively angry personality, people walk and speak gingerly to avoid tripping that wire. They also tend not to think creatively or independently, for fear of being shot down publicly.

• NONVERBAL

It is possible to scream without saying a word. Just ask the people whose bosses give off waves of quiet hostility like nuclear radiation. Nonverbal cues—facial expressions, balled fists, clenched jaw, and sighs—often say as much as a loud voice. In most cases, the hostile person is unaware of their cues. But the rest of the world reads them like a book, and has them completely figured out.

Tim once worked for a boss who said, 'I've never yelled at anybody.' But everyone knew when he was angry whenever his face turned red and he clenched his jaw. Then he became very pedantic and sighed heavily. Employees used to tell him, 'You're screaming at people with your body language!'"

Tish similarly had a client who rubbed his face once when he was upset, and twice when he was angry. The 'double face rub' was something his staff recognized and talked about. It was a company-wide signal, but the client had no idea he was doing it.

• DISAPPOINTMENT

Silent disappointment is deadly, because instead of having the necessary and difficult conversations to express your dissatisfaction directly, you get angry and show your feelings passive-aggressively. Maybe you avoid the people you're angry with. Or you duck key meetings where your nemesis will be present. You might unconsciously postpone or rush decisions on projects that affect that person's business or career. And the most amazing thing about this is that you never tell the subjects of your displeasure why you're unhappy. Which, of course, creates more unhappiness among your staff as they sense your displeasure, but don't know the reason for it and therefore can't do anything about it.

• RESENTMENT

Resentment is anger that simmers for long periods on a low burn. All the while, it's heating up behind the scenes and setting the stage for a full-blown inferno. The resentful leader quietly seethes about subordinates who don't take instruction, people who are promoted without merit, and superiors who aren't fit to carry his or her laptop. The list goes on.

When you feel resentful, consider this. Harboring resentment against someone is like drinking poison and expecting the other person to die.

The Five Real Sources of Anger—They're Not What You Think

It's not your fault that you get so angry. It's not fun for you either. If your people just did what they were supposed to, you wouldn't have to be so ornery, right? Well, not exactly.

Persistent anger, psychologists report, has personal roots. Perennially angry leaders, whether they know it or not, are often angriest with themselves. Steady anger is anguish turned outward. And while the reasons are as individual as people themselves, there are five main sources of anger. The key is to recognize the roots of your anger, have some compassion for yourself, and then work to change the way you think and behave.

- **REGRET**

A relentless sense of discontent with one's life is a tough burden to carry. Perhaps a person lacks educational credentials, and subconsciously spends all day feeling less worthy than colleagues with MBAs from top-tier schools. Maybe he thinks he hasn't been providing for his family the way he should have. Or he's made a few business mistakes that begin gnawing at him whenever the stress level rises. Not making your own mental grade could be causing you to unconsciously take it out on the people around you.

• HANGING ON TO PAST WOUNDS

This is sensitive stuff, but it needs to be said. Even some of the most powerful people have pain in their past, unresolved issues that they may unknowingly be bringing to work. A history with abusive parents, teachers, or clergy can show up as contentious feelings toward people in senior management. A divorce that ended poorly can make a person touchy in situations that are reminiscent of the prior relationship. A devastating experience at a previous job can put someone on constant alert, even when there's no present threat.

• LACK OF SELF-WORTH

Closely related to disappointment as a source of anger is low self-esteem. People with low self-esteem often feel as if they are on the defensive. Every conversation, e-mail, or decision is tinged with the need to prove something. A huge chip on the shoulder can lead to a self-protective display of arrogance, an offensive stance to neutralize perceived attacks. What's interesting is that leaders with low self worth have often "overachieved," and have ample reason to be confident rather than insecure, if only they could see themselves accurately.

• LEARNED BEHAVIOR

People replicate what they've been exposed to, repeating behaviors that appeared successful in other settings. So if you came from a company culture where spiteful behavior was the norm, chances are you'll push that button as a reflex. If you grew up in a family that thrived on dramatic emotional displays, then that's how you learned to meet your needs. But in this instance, imitation is not a sincere or desirable form of flattery. It's a poison that needs to be identified and drained before it taints the rest of the company.

• **FRUSTRATION**

We all get frustrated now and then. When a plum assignment or promotion that you felt should have come your way goes to someone else, it's normal to be upset. But without self-awareness, the distance between frustration and anger is a short ride. That's often the case for people who feel they are trapped in disappointing situations at work or in their personal lives. Being unwilling to take responsibility for the outcomes in your life, preferring to play the victim, can also fuel the fire of anger.

> *Tim Says: Responding to any situation with destructive anger demonstrates a lack of self-awareness and self-control.*

> *Tish Says: This often grows out of people having been victims in their lives. There's an expression: "Hurt people... hurt people."*

HeadTrash Cocktail: Anger with a Control Chaser

Angry people often want to maintain their authority at all costs, and they frequently stir in another HeadTrash: control. They make themselves big and loud in order to dominate the situation. Their presence looms over everything in the office, which was the goal in first place.

An Anger Checklist and Comparison

Which column sounds more like you?

AN ANGRY LEADER...	A CALM LEADER...
Instills fear.	Gains trust.
Gets his way or the highway.	Encourages independent action.
Always has the last word.	Wants to hear what others think.
Makes employees fearful.	Creates a safe environment.
Oversees *everything*.	Delegates responsibility.
Can make the company implode.	Helps the company flourish.
Stifles new thinking.	Fuels innovation.
Keeps people guessing.	Is open and clear on big issues.

HeadTrash Alert! A Quick Quiz on Anger

Please rate yourself on the following statements by placing a checkmark in the appropriate column:

	Never	Sometimes	Often	Always
I think my team tells me what I want to hear.				
If someone performs poorly, I feel the need to "punish" that person.				
I believe I need to yell in order to get my team to perform.				
When someone fails to produce, my first instinct is to get mad.				
I find that people are nervous around me.				
I don't let anybody walk over me. I am ready to fight back, even over small issues.				
After a "situation," I often question if I have overreacted.				
I find myself having to apologize regularly for displays of anger.				

If you checked "often" or "always" three or more times, you probably suffer from anger HeadTrash.

Recognizing the Extremes of Anger: Spontaneous Combustions and Time Bombs

People dealing with anger HeadTrash are often stuck in one of two speeds: instant outbursts or slow-motion implosions. For example, a bad situation triggers you to start shouting or leave an invective-filled voice mail. Or maybe because you couldn't get to the person or a phone fast enough, you think better of flying off the handle. But then you begin to stew—and stew some more. And when that person does something else you disapprove of, you rain the fire of a thousand suns and sins on them.

What's important is to observe your feelings and to avoid either extreme. What's the point of preventing an outburst if you're only going to turn it into a grudge? Watch your feelings and manage them, rather than act on impulse. The trick is to move from enraged accusations to engaged communication. One way to do this is to ask questions instead of attacking the person. For instance, when addressing an employee who has made a mistake with a customer, you could ask specific questions about what happened in the interaction, where things went wrong, and how the situation can be fixed. Typically, the employee will get the message without feeling as if they were attacked. Both parties can leave the conversation prepared to do what they need to do, instead of your feeling enraged and the employee's feeling incapacitated.

Angry Leaders Inspire Fear, Fair Leaders Inspire Loyalty

Fear rides shotgun with anger. It is, after all, how the angry leader often gets his or her way—overtly or with passive-aggressive tactics.

But what happens in a fearful corporate culture after employees initially comply? They often become resentful, and don't trust the leader's future intentions. That motivates them to give just enough effort on any project to keep their jobs. At the first hint of trouble, or a seemingly better offer elsewhere, they're gone faster than you can say HeadTrash.

Conversely, respect's sidecar companion is loyalty. People who feel that they're being treated as equals stick with the leader who values them. They give their best because they want to, because they appreciate the leader who elevates rather than belittles them. Perhaps she's kept her cool and showed restraint in a situation where she may have had reason to be angry. Perhaps he went out of his way to thank someone for a job well done. Such a leader has earned the trust and loyalty of the staff, and will be repaid many times over.

Re: Anger
From the desks of: Marta Martinez, AOL Head of Sales Strategies and Operations, and Tim Myers, Liquid Hub Partner, Insurance Division

Anger can be the nuclear HeadTrash, an emotion so radioactive in the workplace that many business people don't even like to admit they feel it. But as we've said, all the forms of HeadTrash are part of our common humanity. And the people who have the most trouble acknowledging the universal human emotion of anger are also usually the people who are most prone to expressing anger in poisonous and counterproductive ways. The sensation is so powerful, they don't know how to handle it, and their anger boils over and scorches everyone within shouting distance.

But it's okay to feel anger. In fact, it's downright normal, says Tim Myers.

"Being upset is for a reason, right? It's okay to feel whatever you feel, and we need to be able to do that," Meyers says. "But how do you face it in a way that you respectfully say what needs to be said? Being angry doesn't mean you need to tear somebody down."

Marta Martinez agrees that anger happens, and that it should evolve to something more productive. "We're all humans running companies, and humans get angry. So it's okay to feel angry," says Martinez. "You just have to learn how to manage it effectively. And that's what's really hard."

One of the great difficulties of anger is that it often seems to come out of nowhere, hijacking our rational brain and sending us into a state of emotional overload. Something happens. We explode.

But volcanic anger is rarely that simple. A way to start taming this combustible force, says Myers, is to ask yourself, "What caused the blow up? Anger is not a one-horse kind of thing," he says. "It's usually five or six or ten different things, and then—out it comes. Especially when you really lose your temper. It's usually a number of things that trigger the outburst."

So if it's the straw that breaks the camel's back, how should we handle it when the straw lands? While it depends on the situation, Martinez says it's always best to respond from a place of detached neutrality rather than in the heat of the moment. "I have a rule with e-mail. When I get one of those provocative e-mails, I never allow myself to reply right away," she says. "I have to let it settle to be more objective."

The same is true in a public setting. When things get volatile during a meeting, "Never have a group episode," says Martinez. "If you can park it and think about it in two hours, you can deal with the situation more objectively. And then in the calm light of reason, address specific situations, behaviors, or statements, never the person. Don't make it personal."

Meyers adds, "What leaders forget, however, is that they're often responsible for the very episodes that trigger their ill will. For example, why doesn't your staff meet your expectations? Well, maybe because you haven't actually expressed them clearly. For me, expectations in work scenarios can mean the places that we're asking folks to perform in. People miss them because they were never asked. When we don't communicate our expectations, there's no way someone else can live up to them."

But what happens when you actually do define your goals, and your staff consistently fails to meet them? "As a leader, you have to know your people. And you can't expect more from them or different from them than what they're capable of," says Myers. "If you're not capable of relieving that person who isn't doing what they need to do, getting angry at them every day isn't going to make them do it. If they're a known quantity, blowing up is not going to scare them into doing what they can't do."

Myers adds, "Anger is a funny thing. There is no good or bad; there just is. So anger is not a bad thing. It's how you use it, how you feel it, how you communicate it that becomes good or bad, and that's the key for me."

Recommendations for Overcoming the HeadTrash of Anger

FROM ENRAGED ACCUSATIONS TO ENGAGED COMMUNICATION

If you really need some inspiration to control your angry flare-ups, look at your bottom line and your staff. Surely you know how hard it is to attract and keep good people, especially if you've lost a few. Great companies are built around stable management teams who deal with success or adversity with poise and creativity. And that starts with composed, even-keeled leaders. So here are some ways for you to manage the flash fire of anger, before it burns down everything you worked so hard to build.

1. *Breathe.*

   When you feel yourself staring to boil over, stop, breathe, and think before you do or say anything you might regret. Are you so enraged that it might be a good idea to leave the room? Fine, get up and take yourself out of harm's way. Better that than saying or doing something that leaves an indelible mark. Address the issue later, when you're calmer and have thought it through.

2. *Put down the poison pen.*

   In this era of instant communications, it's tempting to bash out an e-mail—emphasis on the word "bash"—to send to the offending party. Don't give into the urge. If you must get it out of your system, go ahead and write the note, *but don't hit the send button.* And don't leave a venomous voice mail. Sleep on it and think about it before you call or write. Even better? Schedule a face-to-face meeting. Difficult topics are always better handled in person, where less is left to interpretation.

3. *Ask yourself, "Am I angry at the situation or at the person?"*
   Even though we're usually angry about the event, we take it
   out on the human being. Making that distinction often has a
   calming effect. If nothing else, it short-circuits an emotional
   overload.

4. *Sort out your thoughts.*
   Now that you're calm and thinking rationally (you are thinking rationally, aren't you?), take a few minutes to write down
   and identify the core issues that are upsetting you. That way
   you can prepare yourself for a productive face-to-face conversation.

5. *Do your homework.*
   As you prep for your talk, remember this is not a "yelling and
   telling" session. Instead, be ready with good questions, and
   work with the other person to resolve the issues.

6. *Language is important.*
   Focus not only on what you want to say, but how you want to
   say it. Phrases like "You should have" or "Why didn't you?"
   or "I am disappointed in you" are accusatory, and will spark
   hostility and defensiveness. Instead ask, "What could we have
   done differently?" "Where were the gaps?" or "How can I help
   you resolve this?" The old standby "Can you help me understand your thinking here?" is a classic line for a good reason:
   it is nonjudgmental, at least if said with sincerity. Unless you
   are a superb actor, the other person will pick up on your in-
   sincerity and the chance for a productive conversation will be
   lost.

7. *Be realistic.*

Do you always perform up to the high standards you hold for yourself? Of course not, and neither does the rest of the world. It is unreasonable to expect people to behave the way you expect in all situations. So don't hold a grudge. Instead, deal with issues in person, before the resentment builds. Once each person has shared his or her point of view, show mutual respect and then move on.

BEHIND THE SCENES WITH TIM & TISH:
ANGER ANECDOTE—A TICKING TIME BOMB

The CEO and founder of an advertising agency had a terrible problem with anger. This ticking time bomb's employees lived in fear of saying or doing the wrong thing. We were introduced to the company by a trusted adviser of the CEO who witnessed a rage-filled explosion at a team meeting when it was learned that the company had just lost a multimillion dollar account to its main competitor. In our first meeting with the CEO, she was still seething with rage, and pointing toward her office door she snarled, "I'm ready to fire them all!" We said we would be happy to work with the staff to improve their performance, but would like to ask a few questions to deepen our understanding of the situation. And so began a two-year consulting relationship that focused on helping the CEO gain control over her emotions.

To the CEO's credit, after a 360-degree emotional intelligence evaluation (the scores for which were quite low), she recognized that her emotions played a major role in the loss of the multimillion dollar contract. It was her anger that increased attrition within the account team, it was her anger that left team members in constant panic over her next attack, and it was her rage that paralyzed the team's performance and ultimately drove the client to the competitor. With this realization she rolled up her sleeves and used all the energy she had spent on anger to work on getting control of her emotions. Over time, there were noticeable improvements at the company: retention of team members improved significantly, as did morale, and the atmosphere was less tense, especially when employees provided feedback to the CEO. There continue to be times when the CEO is challenged by anger. But these times occur less and less frequently. In the few instances when we still have to "pull her off the ceiling," it is not as difficult as in the past and the CEO no longer takes her anger HeadTrash out on her employees.

6

Guilt—Sheathing the Double-Edged Sword

"I have to admit it; I knew she wasn't the best person for the job. But we needed someone in that role, and she was a friend of the family. Six months later, she's not working out the way I had hoped, but I don't feel right about letting her go. Maybe I can bring someone in under her to pick up the areas she's weak on."

—A Leader with Guilt HeadTrash

One of your managers calls you from the road to discuss a meeting he just had with a client. Overall it sounds like it went well enough, and you should be happy. But you realize that you're not processing a thing the guy is saying. Instead there is a distracting noise in your ears.

The manager is talking about how the client is considering taking on new services from the company. How there may be more business coming in from this account. With every word, the noise gets louder and louder, until you finally realize that *the noise is in your head!* It's you, struggling to ignore your inner voice and your own sound judgment, knowing that you should have demoted this guy a year ago when you realized he wasn't cutting it.

Now every time you pass him in the hallway, take his call, or see a message from him in your e-mail, you hear a white hum that keeps you from listening to your own best judgment. And that white hum, believe it or not, is the sound of your own guilt.

For those of us who see ourselves as no-nonsense business directors, titans of industry, and captains of commerce, this particular HeadTrash is a hard thing to accept, let alone identify. So let us begin once again with our trusted third party observer, *Merriam-Webster*, which defines guilt this way.

> **guilt** *noun*
>   *1:* the fact of having committed a breach of conduct especially violating law and involving a penalty; *broadly*: guilty conduct.
>   *2: a* : the state of one who has committed an offense especially consciously
>   *b* : feelings of culpability especially for imagined offenses or from a sense of inadequacy: self-reproach.
>   *3:* a feeling of culpability for offenses

Guilt is such a complicated stew, you may not know where to dip your spoon first. And it is something you can either swallow when it's shoved under your nose or dish out to others. Neither is a productive habit. Another way of saying this is that guilt is a double-edged sword that can greatly damage you and others, depending on how it's wielded against you and by you.

We've stressed that the origin of every HeadTrash is a human emotion or experience that is neither good nor bad in itself. Guilt can be a healthy reaction to mistakes and misdeeds, the spur we need to correct or atone for them. However, failing to resolve guilty feelings as quickly as possible with honest, direct action creates many problems. Running from guilt, wallowing in it, and manipulating other people's guilt are all very unhealthy behaviors. Each is a form of taking the easy way out. It feels better in the short term, but rotten in the long term.

Guilt is the source of sorrow, 'tis the fiend,
Th' avenging fiend, that follows us behind,
With whips and stings.

— Nicholas Rowe, English dramatist
and Poet Laureate (1674–1718)

A Two-Headed Monster: Inflicting Guilt, Feeling Guilt

We couldn't resist one more metaphor for guilt. What makes the two-headed monster of guilt so difficult to deal with is that it's deeply imbedded in us by primal childhood experiences. For many people, it's a vestige of troubled relationships with parents and other authority figures. If we grew up in households or cultural milieus where guilt loomed large, guilty thoughts can play like Muzak in the background for decades, just waiting for the right person to turn up the volume and make us dance. Before we know it, we're thinking, "I am a bad person if I do not speak or behave the way this person wants."

Driven professionals also feel guilty when they don't live up to their own heady ideals or accomplish their lofty goals. This is a particularly common syndrome for people who travel among high achievers and measure themselves harshly against them.

Conversely, if they need someone to do something for them, guilt-ridden leaders often have no compunction about turning the tables and guilt-tripping others. In part this is because we all tend to do unto others as we have been done unto, even if some people with an unhealthy experience of guilt mostly hurt only themselves. But although people who have attained leadership positions may be quite vulnerable in their way, they usually have big enough egos that they can be very dangerous when they feel threatened. The same tactics they may abhor in others become fair game when something meaningful is at stake. In any case, guilt-inflicting leaders are masters at identifying the guilt-ridden, and using guilt like jujitsu to manipulate and exploit them.

Think of it as a coin, and no matter how you flip it, there is no real winner. The guilt you *feel* prevents you from making the right business decision. And the guilt you *wield* gets short-term results at the expense of long-term ill will and fallout.

Guilt is a "gift" that never stops giving—in a poisonous way. To be a successful leader you must learn how to identify guilt, prevent it from ruling your thinking, and avoid using it.

Feeling Guilt versus Offering Compassion

Guilt that we don't confront and resolve directly is a sentimental trap, a snare that hooks us into doing the wrong thing even when we think we're acting out of kindness or benevolence. After all, the people who are underperforming are still worthy of respect as human beings, have families to support, and will suffer if they are dismissed or demoted. The caring thing to do is to keep them right where they are, and find a suitable backdoor solution, right?

Well, no—not if you're doing that involuntarily, and causing grief for others and/or the company as a whole. It's also unfair to keep people in roles that don't fit their skills, when more suitable roles might allow them to blossom.

To get a clearer view of how guilt can go wrong, let's compare acting from misplaced guilt with its healthy cousin, acting from sincere, clear-eyed compassion. Clinging to misplaced guilt is a learned behavior that often encourages us to act against the best interests of the business and the people in it, including ourselves. By contrast, compassion, as defined by *Merriam-Webster*, is a "sympathetic consciousness of others' distress together with a desire to alleviate it."

The key word here is "consciousness." When you are compassionate, you act with awareness and are in control of your feelings. You behave in a caring manner because you choose to, not because you fear that you'll be labeled evil by unseen judges. When you offer an act of compassion, there's no emotional get-out-of-jail card awaiting you. And one of those compassionate acts might be to have some heart-to-hearts with the people in your company who need constructive critiques of their performance.

When you use guilt to pressure someone into doing something, however, you are anything but compassionate.

Symptoms of Guilt-Ridden Leaders

- They postpone decisions to evade stress or conflicts.

- They avoid having the difficult discussions that could promote positive change or end a bad situation.

- They keep people in positions far longer than they should.

- They frequently restructure teams to avoid firing or demoting people, hiding the truth behind new organizational charts.

Symptoms of Guilt-Inflicting Leaders

- The staff works from a sense of obligation rather than ownership, thus giving the minimum amount of effort to any task.

- Employees exhibit a sense of compliance versus commitment. There's not a lot of enthusiasm around the water cooler.

- Instead of assigning tasks to the most appropriate people in order to cultivate new skills and encourage growth, they look for targets they can pressure into doing the job.

- Unhealthy goading and conniving underlie the assignment of projects, making recipients feel manipulated and resentful.

The Far-Reaching Effects of Misplaced Guilt: Five Examples of Unproductive Pain

Like a stone thrown into a pond, misplaced guilt creates profound ripple effects. By avoiding necessary decisions out of a sense of guilt, or using guilt to coerce, the leader often produces unintended consequences.

- *The work-around worker: the staffer everyone avoids*
 Everyone knows that Mary is a horrible manager—everyone but Mary, that is. She has no people skills, and considers her gruff and aloof style "businesslike" and effective. The source of her profound unawareness is her boss, who fifteen years ago hired her as the company's first bookkeeper, and has promoted and shielded her ever since. As the company has grown, he's expanded her responsibilities into roles she's unqualified for—all because he doesn't have the heart to promote people above her.
 The result is that her colleagues do everything in their power to avoid working with her, cutting deals with people in other departments or bringing in consultants to handle projects that could have been done inside. The lost hours of productivity and dollars spent in damage control are through the roof.

• *The apologist: shares credit and roles to avoid hurting others*

Ted and Alice joined the company at the same time in similar roles. Working on companion projects, under the same director, they became friends, and their mutual support helped them both succeed—but not at the same level. Although Ted was competent enough in his initial role, Alice became a company rock star. Senior management rightfully recognized and rewarded her with greatly expanded responsibilities in a series of promotions. Unfortunately for Alice and the company, however, she felt guilty about leaving her buddy Ted behind. She began sending some of her management work his way soon after her first big promotion beyond him, and she has kept that up. She says to herself, "We came in together, and Ted's a great guy. He deserves to get ahead, too." While that may be true, does he deserve Alice's promotions?

• *Compliant workers versus committed team members*

Can't anyone do anything with a smile and some gusto? Would it kill your staff to go the extra mile, even the extra inch, instead of shutting down as soon as the immediate task is "technically" complete? What exactly is going on here? If you're a guilt-wielding director, pushing emotional buttons and using Machiavellian maneuvers to get your people to do your bidding, then you'll get compliance versus commitment. After you've twisted that psychological arm, or turned the mental screws enough to get your way, the person at the receiving end eventually feels used. So when their work is done, so are they. And that sense of investment and excitement you see at other companies is not happening in your own shop.

- *The self-denying superstars: unwilling to own their power and potential*

Lest you ever doubt the potency of guilt, think of how many times you've visited a relative you didn't really want to see or attended a family function against your will because it was the right thing to do, in the words of your mother or your spouse. That kind of guilt trip is but a blip on the radar screen compared to the ways deep-seated, unresolved guilt overrules our best interests. Many highly accomplished executives turn guilt into insurmountable psychological and career obstacles, for fear of outshining a family member or their image of themselves. They may be unable to enjoy their successes because they feel guilty for having gotten as far as they have. Or they may keep themselves stuck in a safe role because the bigger title would bring with it a measure of distinction they think they don't deserve. Although there may be other psychological issues at work, such as a bad case of impostor syndrome, which we discussed earlier in relation to the HeadTrash of insecurity, one part of the equation is guilt at having excelled too much. The saddest part of this kind of guilt is that it's so misguided.

- *The paralyzed leader: loyal to a fault, frozen with regret*

Guilt is so pervasive and insidious that it can pay a compound interest rate, with negative residual returns. Take, for example, the guilt-ridden CEO who finally got up the gumption to change the organizational structure of the company to address the incompetence of a key leader. The new structure effectively demotes this leader. But the CEO announced the restructuring without explaining its rationale to either the staff or the person who was demoted. When the demoted person's performance in the new, diminished role was also unsatisfactory, the CEO elected not to confront the issue. The reason: "I've already hurt this person's career enough." Which means bad performance gets punished without explanation, and without the expectation of change.

Tim Says: Great leadership appeals to logic and emotion—head and heart. Really good leaders get both working for them and earn buy-in from their people.

Tish Says: Guilt-driven leadership plays purely on negative emotions, pulling on the heartstrings versus giving logical reasons why something needs to happen.

A Guilt Checklist and Comparison

Which column sounds most like you?

A GUILT-INFLICTING LEADER...	A GUILT-RIDDEN LEADER...	A COMPASSIONATE LEADER...
Gets his way by exploiting weakness and pushing emotional buttons.	Creates "workarounds" or reassigns people instead of having the difficult conversation.	Makes an honest and compelling case for what really needs to be done.
Seeks, gets, and is content with simple adherence.	Will accept a compromise to avoid conflict.	Inspires commitment among engaged employees.
Appeals to emotions.	Is ruled by emotions.	Has the difficult conversations when needed, and does "the right thing."
By bringing up the past, manipulates others into action.	Avoids the difficult actions and thus puts the business and staff at risk.	Uses the proper communication skills and level of empathy to make the best decision for the business.
Uses guilt to make it difficult for those around the "protected" person to take action.	"Protects" people because he is unwilling to have an uncomfortable conversation.	Acts decisively about promotions or dismissals.
Forces poor performers on other managers or departments, causing great frustration.	Plays musical chairs with people as band-aid solutions that don't solve performance problems.	Recognizes that moving people into roles for which they are unsuited sets them, and the business, up for further failure.

HeadTrash Alert! A Quick Quiz on Guilt

Please rate yourself on the following statements by placing a checkmark in the appropriate column:

	Never	Sometimes	Often	Always
I use "parental guilt" to get my team to deliver on assignments just as I use it to get my children to behave.				
I hold back from making sound business decisions because of personal relationships.				
I rationalize my own bad behaviors (like chewing out an employee in public) by feeling badly long enough to make it okay.				
I use guilt to cajole others to get things done.				
I have "guilted" people into doing things so often in the past that I no longer question whether it is an acceptable tactic.				
I find that I create obstacles to moving forward by reliving past experiences about which I feel badly.				
I feel guilty right now for my answers to these questions.				

If you checked "often" or "always" three or more times, you probably suffer from guilt HeadTrash.

"I've gathered you all here today to tell you how displeased I am with the company's performance. And then to give you all raises for how badly I feel about having to do this."

Beware the Guilt Boomerang: Failed maneuvers take you from one side of guilt to the other

See if this rings a bell. There's a project or a job opening that calls for you to do some serious planning, restructuring, or heavy lifting. But you don't feel like going through all the effort. And in your search for an easier solution, you land on a compromise— one that requires you to do some emotional wheeling and dealing to get a subordinate to take on a role that doesn't suit her, but gets you out of the jam. Your guilt trip works, and the person accepts, despite being an ill-fitting square peg.

Jump ahead eighteen months, and what do you know? It's not working out. That poor soul is in over her head, and you're too guilty to do anything because you begged, borrowed, and stole her pride to put her in this spot.

The guilt boomerang comes back to haunt many a leader because a person pushed into the wrong place rarely finds a way to make it work. And the one who pushed her rarely has the courage to admit they were wrong twice.

Re: Guilt
From the desk of: Erika Weinstein, president of Stephen-Bradford Search

As a businessperson, Erika Weinstein has nothing to feel guilty about in our view. She's the president of Stephen-Bradford Search, the successful Manhattan-based executive search firm she co-founded. She's been responsible for hundreds of high-profile placements, including positions for companies like Disney, Coca-Cola, American Express, and Pitney Bowes. Yet Weinstein says that one of the HeadTrashes she most identifies with is guilt.

For example, there are the instances when a company has to let someone go. "But then you think, 'Well, Jane just had surgery. This is not a good time,'" she says. "And then Christmas comes along, and you don't want to be a schmuck and let her go right before Christmas. Now six months of inactivity have gone by because this employee wasn't right for the job. But you're still feeling sorry for her about putting her out on the street."

And guilt is not just an emotion associated with painful decisions. It's also a tool, says Weinstein, a lever people pull to get what they want. "Guilt is used in so many clever ways in business. You guilt people into calling you back. Or you guilt people into doing things your way. People are always guilting each other in business. It's very powerful."

To make the point, Weinstein uses the example of a guilt-driven sales pitch. "Let's say I'm golfing with Sam, my friend of twenty years. He asks me why he didn't win my business on his last bid. He tells me it's his third time bidding us," Weinstein says. "So I'm feeling bad about this, and now I'm going to award him the project—even though, by the way, Sam should not have been awarded the business the first time, the second time, or now! That's playing the guilt card."

We're all susceptible, says Weinstein. It's normal, it's human. When we try to protect an employee's income and self-esteem by not firing him or her, we show our compassion, our desire to do right by the person. Protecting people can be a mistake, however, if firing them really *is* the right thing to do—for them as well as everyone else.

"The truth of the matter is I'm not doing that person or the business a good service if they're not right for the job. They need to have this door closed in order for another door to open," says the woman whose job it is to open the right doors for the right people.

Extenuating circumstances may well be an appropriate consideration in the timing of dismissals or demotions, but good leaders have the courage to plan and follow through on such moves when they are right for the business. It's not always Christmas, after all.

Recommendations for Overcoming the HeadTrash of Guilt

How do you stop manipulating and/or being manipulated with guilt, and start practicing direct conversation and action? Like all habit change, it's not easy, but it is doable. Start with being clear about the principles you want to follow.

1. *Move on quickly.*
   Lingering guilt is the mind's way of trying to rewrite history and change the outcome, which of course is impossible. What's done is done, and no matter how many times you think about it or try to resolve it differently, nothing will change. Instead, drop the baggage, hit the pedal, and move forward with your life and your career.

2. *Stop manipulating and maneuvering.*
   Yes, emotional blackmail can be effective in the short term to get others to do your bidding. But the pain is not worth the gain, and you will never grow as a leader. Instead, practice your influence skills by helping others see the importance of accomplishing business goals. Motivate rather than manipulate, and meet challenges head on with direct solutions.

3. *Talk it out.*
   Feeling guilty about something you said or did? Instead of stewing in your guilt soup, have a conversation with the person you feel you've wronged. Guilt can be a legitimate initial emotion, but it becomes troublesome when we hang on it.

4. *Learn from history.*
   Vow not to repeat it. The best thing you do can after the fact

is to try to understand why you behaved the way you did, and then commit to not repeating the mistake. It's a way of taking control versus staying stuck in the past.

BEHIND THE SCENES WITH TISH & TIM: GUILT ANECDOTE—FRIENDSHIP GETS IN THE WAY

We once worked with a seasoned CEO at his third company, a mobile technology firm that needed leadership changes because of its own rapid growth as well as increased competition in the marketplace. However, unhealthy guilt was getting in the way. The CEO was determined to keep a senior leader in a role that he simply was not qualified to perform as the company expanded, because the individual in question was a personal friend who had been with the company since its inception. This caused serious problems not only in the friend's area of responsibility, but in the functioning of the company's entire senior management team. The company's other leaders had all lost confidence in the CEO's friend, and they were steadily losing confidence in the CEO, too.

It was not easy for the CEO to consider making the necessary moves and have the necessary discussions with his friend about the change. It required discipline, focus, and confidence that the goodwill and trust built over the years would see both men through the transition. With help, however, the CEO was able to create an effective development plan for his friend that involved transferring him into a more appropriate position. The plan reduced the CEO's misplaced guilt so that he could take action that was long overdue.

We reminded the CEO throughout the process that guilt is a healthy, appropriate response when we have done something wrong or hurt another, but that misplaced guilt over his friend was not in the best interests of either the friend or the business. After the CEO moved the leader into a position at the company that suited his skills better, his effectiveness in the new role allowed him to regain credibility with the other members of the leadership team. The move also renewed the rest of the leadership team's faith in the CEO, which was crucial to keeping the company on its fast growth track.

When you have a misaligned leader, it's very important to create small wins when transitioning him or her to a new role. You'll get much better results by seeking to increase the leader's credibility step by step rather than by trying to pull off a major transformation all at once.

"Step by step" is a good motto for all HeadTrash-related change. Rome wasn't built in a day, and healthy mental and emotional patterns will also take time to establish. The last form of HeadTrash we want to discuss, paranoia, exemplifies that.

7

Paranoia—Replacing Anxiety and Suspicion with Confidence and Trust

"As one of the leaders in my company, I think it's prudent to be cautious. After all, that's what keeps my division out of trouble, and keeps me ahead of the pack. It's just that I see things differently because other people are too casual about running a business. I know I spend a lot of time micromanaging. But that's a price I'm willing to pay to make sure things don't go wrong, even if it's difficult to keep up with everything all the time."

—A Leader with Paranoia HeadTrash

There was a lot riding on the presentation, so it would be natural for anyone to be a little gun-shy while preparing for the big day. Worrywart that you are, you had thought everything through, building the pitch around a sound strategy that addressed the central issues in the request for proposals.

Your diligence seemed to pay dividends. The second you finished presenting your slide deck and closed your computer, the prospect said, "I think these are great solutions. It's obvious that you put a great deal of energy and thinking into this. I just need to think about how best to sell this upstairs to senior management."

Back at the office, everyone on the team agreed that it was an exceptional pitch, and that you in particular were on your game.

But something wasn't right for you; something triggered your radar detector. It was that moment during the meeting when one of the client's managers asked a question about how you would implement the program. "How can you make this less complicated?" she asked.

You were ready for it, of course, answering the challenge smoothly. That got a nod out of the questioner, and the meeting moved on. The way the prospect nodded, however, left you unsatisfied, doubting the manager had bought your answer. The doubt quickly grew into certainty that she was not convinced, and that this would spell doom for your pitch. Didn't anyone else notice it?

Actually, no, because you have such a highly developed sense of paranoia, you convinced yourself that good news was bad, despite the facts before your eyes.

When we hear the word "paranoia," we tend to think of a clinical psychological disorder, which is how *Merriam-Webster* describes it in its first definition. But the word also has a more general meaning.

> *paranoia* noun
> *1:* a psychosis characterized by systematized delusions of persecution or grandeur usually without hallucinations
> *2:* a tendency on the part of an individual or group toward excessive or irrational suspiciousness and distrustfulness of others

For our purposes, it's the second definition that captures how paranoid leaders often behave in the workplace, especially the phrase "irrational suspiciousness and distrustfulness of others." Of course, if you're paranoid, you're probably thinking, "Irrational!?!?

How can it be irrational if it's true?" Well, that's the point. We all know the joking line, "Just because you're paranoid doesn't mean they aren't out to get you." But as George and Ira Gershwin wrote, "It ain't necessarily so."

The e-mail you think is filled with veiled threats, or the business meeting you thought was a precursor to your getting fired—in the overwhelming majority of cases the "evidence" paranoid people use to justify their concerns doesn't actually exist. It's fiction, a self-invented story written from a script that begins and ends from his or her point of view on everything. And in the rare instances where there are some facts that would rightfully cause concern, the paranoid person will take a small kernel of truth and pump enough fear into it to create a whole ear of corn.

Paranoia versus Insecurity:
I Doubt You versus I Doubt Myself

It would be natural to think that suspicious business leaders imagine others feel negatively or hostilely towards them, because the people they most doubt are themselves, and their insecurity leads them to feel fearful. A lack of self-confidence can cause anyone to see the glass as half empty all the time.

But the paranoid person sees the glass not only as half empty, but also as spiked with hemlock. It's a mind-set that makes paranoid business leaders distrust every situation and most people. It expresses their absolute certainty that people are out to get them.

Most people, for example, would be delighted to learn that one of their bosses had publicly championed an idea of theirs, and given them credit for the idea during an executive team meeting. From that information one might reasonably conclude that they had scored major points with their immediate superior, who then spread the love to the rest of the company's management team.

Believing that they're unworthy of such compliments, insecure people may feel that the boss was simply taking pity on them. But the paranoid person wonders what the boss's real agenda was. "Why did he suddenly decide to praise my idea? And what did he mean by saying it was a 'good interim answer to a problem no one else could solve?'" The paranoid person always looks for a hidden intention.

> "I moved to New York City for my health. I'm paranoid,
> and it was the only place where my fears were justified."
> —Anita Weiss

Paranoia: The Distorted Lens that Taints Everything

As with every other type of HeadTrash, the paranoid person brings his special set of panic goggles to every situation. He doesn't need a precipitating cause to arouse suspicion because it's there all the time, operating in the background. Did someone ask you to write a report about a project you're wrapping up? Well, clearly that person is out to get you. What are they going to do with the report, and how will it reflect on you? Was a meeting held without you while you were on vacation? That can't be good, because it gave people an opportunity to talk behind your back and advance their plans ahead of yours.

This perennial state of victimhood stands in the way of getting things done, and is usually draining for the paranoid person scrambling to put a finger in every perceived leak. It also saps the people around him, who are running around with the hoses, attempting to extinguish the paranoid's fictional fires. This malady can actually increase as one rises to more senior positions. The more senior the role, the more isolated a leader can feel, because being at the helm of a business requires a certain level of separation from "the troops." As the old saying goes, "It's lonely at the top," and it is not uncommon for folks in such a position to become suspicious. A classic example from history of a leader whose suspiciousness got the best of him is President Richard Nixon, whose paranoia led him directly into the Watergate controversy. Nixon got so good at convincing himself of his paranoid thoughts that his behaviors killed his credibility and ultimately brought down his presidency.

Two Types of Paranoid Responses: I Do Everything; I Do Nothing.

The internal experience of business paranoia, obsessive worry about non-factual events and perceived threats, is similar for most executives who wrestle with it. But its external effects—how it manifests itself in their behavior—can be very different.

For some, paranoia is a rocket launcher that drives them into hyperactive mode to cover their tracks and manage conversations, setting multiple events into motion continually. Tim has a client who is constantly reacting to perceived slights to his department or him personally. He's like the circus performer who is trying to keep all the plates in the air. Even though this person is good at his job, and has a good reputation, he's exhausted all the time.

On the flip side are leaders whose paranoia prevents them from doing anything at all. Their thoughts paralyze them to the point that they cannot make a productive decision. They avoid taking a stand on anything, so as not to give anyone ammunition against them.

Symptoms of a Paranoid Leader

• Genuinely believes that others are out to get him, and lives in a constant state of victimhood.

• Is obsessed with what others are going to think, and spends a great deal of time on image management.

• Is certain every e-mail has a potentially negative connotation.

• Views requests for information as threats, pondering what the receiver will do with the data, and how it will reflect on her.

• Perceives personal slights everywhere, interpreting conversational miscues as deliberate snubs and passing glances as dirty looks. What others brush off, this person obsesses about.

• When an e-mail, phone call, or other communication does not occur as expected, immediately assumes he or she did something wrong.

Paranoia at work:
Undermining Success in So Many Ways

To a surgeon, the entire world is a scalpel. To a paranoid business leader, everyone is the enemy, which means that every decision, interaction, or exchange is fraught with danger. Unable to look beyond his distrust long enough to do what's right in each situation, he damages the company by putting his interests and worries first.

- *Hiring weak employees to avoid being upstaged.* The paranoid manager can't bring herself to hire a strong performer for fear that others on the team will like the new hire better than her. Should a talented candidate happen to slip past the paranoid's radar, she will subject their every action to CIA-level scrutiny for fear of being outshined.

- *Causing unnecessary drama.* Paranoids talk up their fears, looking for validation of their worldview. Unfortunately, it's the kind of conversation that creates sideshows and theatrics, distracting people from their real work. A statement like "Did you see the way he reacted to me this morning?" can ripple out into rumors, ill will, and distractions, all of which drag down performance.

- *Negating a collaborative environment.* In the book *The Five Dysfunctions of a Team,* by Patrick Lencioni, dysfunction *numero uno* is the absence of trust among team members. Paranoid leaders are incapable of inspiring trust because they can't evoke in others what they don't have themselves. Their innate doubt of each person's motives prevents them from creating a collegial, focused team, supporting each other to work toward a common cause.

HYPERACTIVITY VERSUS PRODUCTIVITY

By focusing on politics and hearsay, the paranoid channels energy toward intrigue and hysterics at the expense of productive work. It's CYA (Cover Your Assets) every day, all day.

- *No risk, no reward.* Not surprisingly, paranoid people are afraid to take risks, second and third guessing every decision and action. While a little caution is healthy, paranoid people can't get out of their own way to reach a conclusion and move forward. As any veteran business leader knows, you can't get around the bases if you're unwilling step off of first.

- *It's all about me and my worries.* Paranoid people are high maintenance. Their supervisors and colleagues must work overtime to rebut their cherished conspiracy theories, and talk them down from imagined ledges. This robs hours from the development of other people in the company.

> *Tish Says: Just because someone is paranoid, that doesn't mean they are not good at their job. They can be, but they allow obsessed negativity to cause them to think they are not, or that someone has it in for them.*

> *Tim Says: Others turn paranoia into an asset. I've seen people who are political animals, overhearing something and then rushing around like mad to address it, and make it look good. And then play the other side, too. But it eats them up inside.*

A Paranoia Checklist and Comparison

Which column sounds more like you?

A PARANOID LEADER...	A TRUSTING—AND TRUSTWORTHY—LEADER...
Is jealous of the success of other people, for fear of being outshone.	Celebrates wins and feels there are enough kudos to go around.
Is always suspicious.	Is appropriately cautious.
Micromanages every situation.	Empowers team members to work autonomously to achieve goals.
Has trouble building team loyalty because they provide only limited information.	Prefers informed, confident, and engaged team members.
Is guarded and can be combative if experiencing a perceived threat.	Is direct, open, and emotionally balanced.
Frequently changes direction for self protection.	Makes decisions and follows through on plans and promises.

HeadTrash Alert! A Quick Quiz on Paranoia

Please rate yourself on the following statements by placing a checkmark in the appropriate column:

	Never	Sometimes	Often	Always
At least once per day, I spend time worrying about what others are thinking about me.				
I hang on to feelings of resentments long after other parties say they've moved on.				
When I am not invited to a meeting, I obsess over why I was not included.				
When I am part of a team, I resist sharing my thoughts and feelings because they will be used against me.				
When others say, "Hey, I've heard a lot about you!" I automatically panic and think the worst.				
Even after being assured that "all is well," I continue to worry that it is not.				
I misinterpret friendly teasing or kidding around as a personal attack.				

If you checked "often" or "always" three or more times, you probably suffer from paranoia HeadTrash.

"My supervisor just told me that I got a promotion and a raise. Not to be paranoid, but what do you think she meant by that?"

Re: Paranoia
From the desks of Phil Clemens, chairman and CEO of Hatfield Quality Meats and Chris Saridakis, CEO of GSI Commerce

At the mere mention of paranoia, Phil Clemens, chairman and CEO of Hatfield Quality Meats, is off and running, describing in rich detail how he's seen it cause peers and subordinates to scheme and quake in their corner offices.

Paranoia, says Clemens, has leaders "fighting battles that will never exist. They actually think they're being proactive." These executives "believe their ruminations are leading somewhere. They first get the thought, and they keep developing it. They build it and build it."

What begins as a supposition quickly becomes a fact, confirming what all paranoids know: the world really is out to get them, and the rest of us are just too blind to see it. The blind spot, of course, actually resides in the eye of the beholder, because few HeadTrashes are as narcissistically motivated as paranoia, says Chris Saridakis, CEO of GSI Commerce.

"Generally people who are in decision-making roles with this form or HeadTrash make every issue into something about themselves," says Saridakis. Their actions and thought process are self-focused, "rather than about the position or the company or the problems they're trying to solve. If they're paranoid about their current role or position or something else, it could be hurtful to the company, but they don't see it."

Speaking to the same point, Clemens describes working with an executive who "had a paranoia that had to do with lawsuits. He looked at everything in his business and said, 'Can I get sued for doing this?' He had a real fear." So real, it stopped him from taking any action at all. In his zeal to protect the company, he was preventing it from growing, stopped in his tracks by imaginary legal problems. "I reminded him that people can always sue you, whether it's legitimate or not." Working with the executive, Clemens helped him adopt a new attitude of "If it comes we'll deal with it, but I won't allow me to make me paranoid." Clemens reminded him that he had to drive the business and ignore the noise in his head.

But what explains the paranoia paradox? What causes some of the most powerful people in the company to become the most suspicious? Saridakis agrees that, as we noted earlier, leaders can suffer a lot from its being "lonely at the top." Some people become overloaded with anxiety as their authority increases. "This can be a natural reaction to rising up the ranks in a company," says Saridakis.

Recommendations for Overcoming the HeadTrash of Paranoia

FROM BELIEVING THE NOISE IN YOUR HEAD TO SORTING OUT THE FACTS.

Paranoid reactions are deeply ingrained, and the person who suffers from them oftentimes has a great challenge moving beyond them. This is particularly true for leaders whose modus operandi of circumventing every perceived threat with a paranoid response appears to be working in their favor. Why change now?

The reason, of course, is for the health of the business and your peace of mind. The world of the paranoid executive is unhappy and terrified by definition. Danger lurks where none is present. Small concerns are magnified to five-alarm blazes. And compliments or expansions of responsibility are viewed with suspicion. Imagine how much better life would be if you could learn to relax a little and see things more clearly.

Here are practical suggestions we have found useful in helping paranoid executives learn to interrupt paranoid thought processes, substitute a more productive way of thinking, and restructure their leadership habits to be both more effective in their work and easier in their own skins.

1. *Check your thoughts with a trusted adviser.*
   Easier said than done, because paranoids trust few people enough to hear what they're saying back to them. That is why

it's essential that you cultivate a trusted listener, a higher angel who recognizes your flawed thinking and can give you the real scoop. This is someone you should turn to regularly to help you sort the fact from the fiction. Because you believe this person has your best interests in mind, and understands your business, you may actually take their words to heart.

BEHIND THE SCENES WITH TISH & TIM: PARANOIA ANECDOTE—THE REALITY CHECK

In one instance, we coached a vice president of sales in a highly competitive client services company. This leader had been with the company eight years and excelled in his role, but recently the board had brought in a new CEO from outside the industry who had a process-driven style. The VP of sales was anything but process driven. He was high-touch, emotional, sociable, and needed lots of approval, which he had received regularly from the previous CEO. Almost immediately paranoia set in and the VP of sales became convinced that his new boss didn't like him and was going to move him out of the company. Having worked on the integration of the new CEO with the leadership team, we saw no empirical data to suggest this paranoia was warranted. We noticed the new CEO's process orientation and desire to know only the facts. Whether the company was hitting its metrics, maintaining a full pipeline, and pricing products per established guidelines were the CEO's main concerns, and he was in fact somewhat lacking as regards the emotional intelligence side of leadership.

We shared our perspective with the VP of sales, but it wasn't enough to assuage his paranoia. He continued to feel that there was too little recognition of his and his team's achievements, and that this had to portend dire consequences sooner or later.

As a way to break through this paranoia, the first thing we did was to encourage the VP of sales to recognize his own behavioral style and compare it to the CEO's. There was an immediate "aha!" moment when the VP realized that the situation was not being driven by any dislike of him on the CEO's part, but was rather a difference of style. The two leaders came at things from opposite directions.

After this we provided regular reinforcement to the VP of sales each time he felt upset by the CEO's approach. We helped the VP to look at each situation rationally. Countless times we found ourselves saying, "Now wait a minute, let's take a look at this…." Over time the VP became desensitized to the imaginary slights and threats he was perceiving. His confidence went back up, and the paranoid episodes decreased.

2. *Write it out before you blurt it out.*

Before you explode over a perceived slight to your status, go back to your office and ask yourself, "Why am I feeling this way?" It's remarkable how sitting quietly with your thoughts and a blank piece of paper or computer screen helps you sort out your emotions. Away from the event, you may find that you were misreading the situation through your own interpretations of fear and doubt.

3. *Don't assume, ask for clarity.*

Before you allow a paranoid line of thought to run away with you, speak up. If possible, ask the person or group involved what they were thinking. You might be surprised to learn that you were concerned unnecessarily.

4. *Learn to accept a compliment and take "yes" for an answer.*

Seriously, learn how to accept praise for a change instead of looking for the dark side of a pat on the back. Instead of wondering what someone meant by complimenting your work or agreeing with your proposal, take your kudos at face value. The simple act of accepting a compliment (not so simple for you, actually) may teach you how to see and accept things as they are, rather than as your feelings distort them.

5. *Note situations that trigger suspicious thoughts.*
Although you probably view all situations through the same frame of reference, specific events may trigger a heightened sense of mistrust. Keep a log of what set you off, and a pattern may emerge illustrating your paranoia hotspots: requests for information, certain people, preparations for presentations, etc. Once you're aware of what causes you to become defensive, you can work to combat and question your thinking.

As we've explored throughout this book, the starting point to overcoming any really challenging HeadTrash is to learn how to short circuit and reinterpret your thinking. Thoughts, powerful and personal though they may be, are not facts. They're opinions, feelings, and suppositions, and subject to error.

When HeadTrash Is No Longer the Boss of You

Fear, arrogance, insecurity, control, anger, guilt, and paranoia—these "demons" can derail even the most promising leaders. That is why we wrote this book, to deliver a warning and a promise.

The warning is that when leaders' HeadTrash goes unaddressed, it can have a profoundly negative impact on them, their teams, and their whole businesses. The ash heap of corporate America is piled high with the victims of HeadTrash: leaders who've failed to recognize their shortcomings until it was too late; followers who were too traumatized to care; and businesses that lost talent and profits.

The promise is that when you recognize you have a form of HeadTrash, and are willing to do the work to overcome it, you can be an exemplary leader. Having the self-awareness to admit you have a problem is always the first step toward transformation. Working diligently to learn how to change your thoughts and behaviors will improve your life, and the lives of those in your charge. And you'll see the effects on your business in the bottom line. We've witnessed extraordinary transformations in leaders previously imprisoned by bad business behaviors, captains who've accomplished amazing things, with followers willing to go to hell and back for them. This can be your legacy as well, *if* you're willing to work at it.

That's our promise to you.

And let us remind you once again of the most important fact. *It's okay to have HeadTrash!* More than that, it's unavoidable. To some degree we all have HeadTrash in one form or another. Your HeadTrash doesn't mean you're damaged goods; it means you're human. But if you're leading a company, a division—even a small staff—it's your responsibility to recognize when corrosive thought patterns are damaging you leadership, and then to figure out how to manage them.

Also, we want to note that the seven forms of HeadTrash we've discussed are the most common ones we see in the business world. The list is not intended to be exhaustive, but to point out the obstacles you're most likely to encounter as you pursue your goals in business and in life.

So view this book not as a one-and-done, but as a resource to return to repeatedly. Highlight it! Take the HeadTrash quizzes. Use it to challenge our assumptions and your own. Perhaps it will spur you to secure an executive coach who can work with you to take on your particular challenges, providing the tools you'll need to think and behave differently. The point is to try new approaches, and not be afraid to fail. Be willing to begin your voyage of self-development to transform your leadership approach and everything it touches.

No doubt the journey will be difficult at times, but the payoff will be extraordinary. We promise you that, too.

As any great leader knows, the best thing you can do for your staff and your business is to bring them along for the ride. Once you've learned how to manage your own HeadTrash, you'll want to help others on your team identify their mental baggage, and enable them to become the powerhouses you knew they could be when you hired them. This book will help you work with your staff on their development.

We will be offering further perspective on HeadTrash-related matters on our website and blog, HeadTrash911.com, in future books, and in our seminar, "HeadTrash: Sweep It, Bag It, Crush It!" To close, we'd like to give you a capsule description of the seminar that also serves as a summary of this book.

HeadTrash: Sweep It, Bag It, Crush It!

SWEEP IT—The first step on the path to being a more effective leader is to identify your personal HeadTrash and sweep it into the center of your consciousness. This awareness alone will help you begin to manage unwanted behaviors. But sweeping up HeadTrash is demanding work. It requires an open mind and a strong character to recognize your own HeadTrash: emotional honesty about who you are, and the fortitude to be willing to change.

BAG IT—Once you've identified and accepted your Head-Trash, it's time to eliminate it and put it where it belongs. But before you bag HeadTrash like lawn clippings or fall leaves, you need to have a greater understanding of how it exhibits itself and the negative impact it can have on you and your effectiveness as a leader. Bagging it signifies that you have been able to contain and isolate the counterproductive emotional and mental patterns that generate HeadTrash. Bagging it means learning to recognize situations where your HeadTrash may come into play, defusing the situation before it becomes problematical, and replacing Head-Trash behavior with more appropriate, productive behavior.

CRUSH IT—Crushing old behaviors takes discipline, desire, and determination. But once you finally rid yourself of success-limiting emotional and mental patterns, you will for the first time be able to maximize your skills and utilize your talents to their fullest potential. And then you can truly crush it!

We hope you'll join us in an ongoing conversation about the challenges and rewards of resolving HeadTrash problems. In the meantime, we urge you to *sweep it, bag it, crush it!*

ABOUT THE AUTHOR: TISH SQUILLARO

"I can't imagine there isn't a way. Everything is achievable."

—*Tish Squillaro*

With this goal-oriented and self-confident mind-set, Tish creates change. With an instinctual feeling for niche markets and a talent for helping business leaders become "unstuck" and teaching them to make effective decisions, she drives success by focusing her time and commitment to CANDOR Consulting, advising executives with her bold style of training and guidance. She warns clients early: "If you don't feel differently about how you are making decisions after 30 days, I'm doing something wrong."

Tish helps clients leverage human capital to *drive* the success of their businesses rather than simply support it. Drawing on a wealth of knowledge from a broad range of disciplines, she has particular expertise in change management processes, business strategy development, and behavioral and organizational dynamics. Combining sharp problem-solving skills with effective mediation abilities, Tish works primarily with CEOs, executive managers, and boards of directors within organizations at various stages of development, ranging from start-ups to Fortune 500 companies.

The idea for *HeadTrash* was born while Tish was advising a client who was immobilized by fear, guilt, and insecurity. Seeing the fear of failure in her client's eyes was Tish's first personal "HeadTrash" experience. As she was developing her business,

Tish often needed other people's confirmation to bolster her self-confidence and rise above insecurity. Learning to manage this type of HeadTrash, which she defines as "patterns of self-defeating feelings and thoughts that can immobilize and keep you stuck," has made her a sought-after adviser to executives and CEOs of companies like GSI Commerce/Ebay, ESAB, and *USA Today*.

Tish is the CEO and Managing Partner of CANDOR Consulting. She is a graduate of the University of Pennsylvania and is a member of the Board of Directors of the Philadelphia-based nonprofit organization ACHIEVEability. Tish lives with her husband and two children in Valley Forge, PA.

ABOUT THE AUTHOR: TIM THOMAS

Timothy I. Thomas began his work in leadership consulting in 2003 as a natural outgrowth of his educational background and his life-long commitment to helping others succeed. Tim is a 1987 graduate from of the University of Akron and holds two masters degrees: a M.Div. from Princeton Theological Seminary (1990), and a M.S. in Training and Organization Development from Saint Joseph's University in Philadelphia (2002).

As the Founding Partner of Makarios Consulting, LLC, Tim has helped to transform organizations since 1998 as a leadership development trainer, executive coach, and change management expert. Tim has extensive expertise in the design and delivery of training programs, executive coaching, performance consulting, team development, and 360-degree appraisal processes. He brings clients a complete understanding of corporate culture and business processes as well as keen financial acumen, having himself been a vice president at two international banking institutions.

Known for his highly energetic and engaging facilitation style and his strong commitment to helping his clients realize their full potential, Tim has trained or coached hundreds of leaders in the art of influencing others and achieving extraordinary results, both in business and in life. *HeadTrash* is his current vehicle for transforming lives.

HeadTrash is the first book in the HeadTrash series. Forthcoming books by the authors include:

- *HeadTrash: For Sales People Who Want to WIN*
  (due in stores winter 2014)
- *HeadTrash: College Grads Succeeding in the Workforce*
  (due in stores spring 2014)
- *HeadTrash: Navigating Relationships*
  (due in stores winter 2015)